1986 edition published by Derrydale Books, distributed by Crown
Publishers, Inc.

Library of Congress Cataloging-in-Publication Data

Scarry, Huck.
   Things that go.

   Translation of: Lo sai come si viaggia?
   Summary: Explains scientific and ''day to day''
reasons behind what makes things such as cars and trains
go.
   1. Engines — Juvenile literature.   [1. Engines.
2. Transportation]   I. Title
TJ250.S3313   1986   629.04'9   85-29355
ISBN 0-517-61655-6

h g f e d c b a

Printed in Spain by Artes Gràficas Toledo S.A.
D. L. TO: 331 -1986

Huck Scarry

Things that Go

Derrydale Books
New York

The World on Wheels

Can you imagine a world without transportation? Nothing would move. You would not be able to go see a friend. It would be impossible to go to the movies. You would be unable to go buy an ice cream! What a contrast to the world we live in today!

Indeed, every day, you go to school. How do you get there? Do your feet take you, or do you go by bus? Does your father drive to work, or does he ride a bike? And when mother brings home groceries, how does she do it?

You see, we use transportation every day. We move about so much, on foot, by bicycle, by automobile, by bus, by train, that we hardly give these wonderful means of transport a second thought!

But do you really know how you walk? What keeps your bicycle from falling while you ride? How does a car's engine work? You don't know? Then turn the pages! Let's take a look and see what makes things go.

Friction increases as the weight of an object increases. Twice as much effort is required to move a weight of 20 pounds, as a weight of 10 pounds. That is why it takes tremendous energy to drag a stone block, weighing several tons, across the ground.

Much of the friction between rubbing surfaces can be eliminated by reducing the area of the sliding surfaces and improving them. Ancient Egyptian builders moved heavy stones on wooden sleds, reducing the friction surfaces to just the area of the sled runners. Friction could be further eliminated by laying wooden sleepers for the sled to be dragged over. The heat built up by the rubbing wooden surfaces was quenched by watering the sleepers in front of the sled.

Sled on track

Friction: Friend and Foe

Any objects moving against one another resist each other. This resistance is called friction. Because friction in many ways impedes movement, man, throughout history, has devised methods of overcoming it by using sleds, rollers, and wheels.

Friction can waste a lot of energy, building up heat between any moving parts. Tiny rollers or cylinders, called bearings, are placed liberally in machinery wherever friction is a problem, while lubricants such as oil and grease allow any sliding parts to move easily. Frequent lubrication is necessary to keep any machine in good, working order.

But friction is also a good friend. Without it, we would be unable to move! It allows us to adhere to the ground with our feet, letting us push ourselves forward. All rolling wheels adhere to some surface to move along. Friction also permits us to stop, once in motion. After the wheel, the brake is the most important part of any rolling vehicle!

Sled on rollers

Rolling friction is much less important than sliding friction, so progress can be greatly improved by placing mobile rollers under the sled. The final improvement would be, of course, to mount the sled on wheels. Rollers of one sort or another are found in almost all machinery, wherever two moving parts come into contact with one another. These are called bearings. The most common bearings are ball bearings and roller bearings, which allow two parts to glide past one another with a minimum of friction.

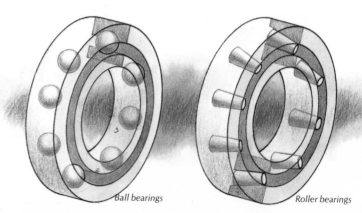

Ball bearings   *Roller bearings*

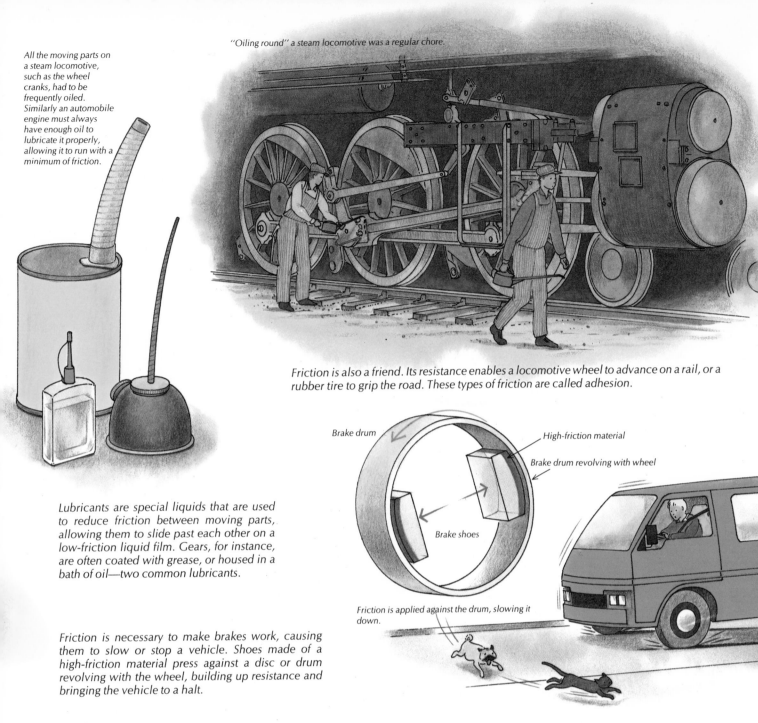

All the moving parts on a steam locomotive, such as the wheel cranks, had to be frequently oiled. Similarly an automobile engine must always have enough oil to lubricate it properly, allowing it to run with a minimum of friction.

"Oiling round" a steam locomotive was a regular chore.

Friction is also a friend. Its resistance enables a locomotive wheel to advance on a rail, or a rubber tire to grip the road. These types of friction are called adhesion.

Lubricants are special liquids that are used to reduce friction between moving parts, allowing them to slide past each other on a low-friction liquid film. Gears, for instance, are often coated with grease, or housed in a bath of oil—two common lubricants.

Brake drum

High-friction material

Brake drum revolving with wheel

Brake shoes

Friction is applied against the drum, slowing it down.

Friction is necessary to make brakes work, causing them to slow or stop a vehicle. Shoes made of a high-friction material press against a disc or drum revolving with the wheel, building up resistance and bringing the vehicle to a halt.

Snow and ice have surfaces that offer little friction, making it easy to sled, to ski, or to skate. But the lack of friction on ice may make walking on it a painful experience!

Natural Locomotion

Imagine if you couldn't move! You could never go out or meet anyone. We tend to take movement for granted, yet it is one of the miracles of the animal world. Movement is a faculty all animals share, and nature has provided for it in a great variety of ways. Such movement is called natural locomotion, and some examples of this are shown below.

Walking

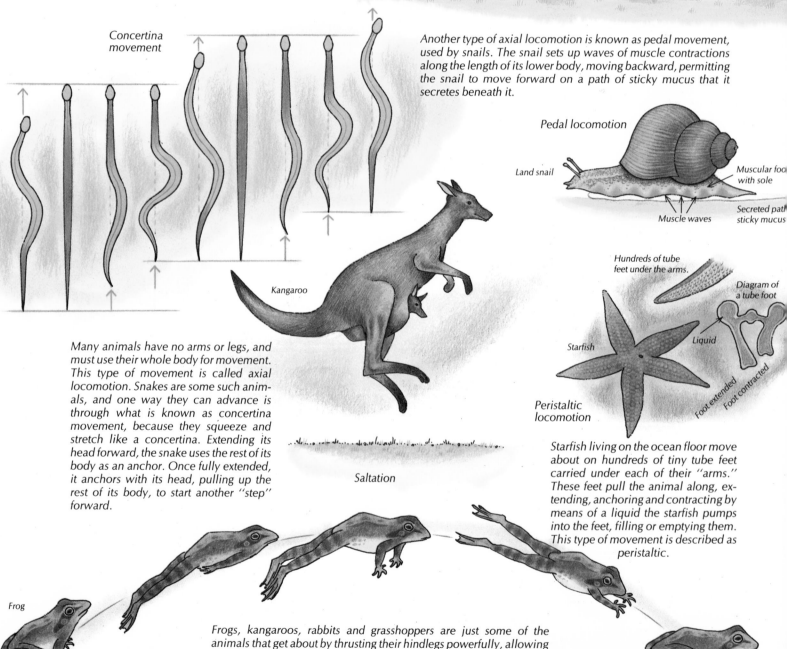

Concertina movement

Another type of axial locomotion is known as pedal movement, used by snails. The snail sets up waves of muscle contractions along the length of its lower body, moving backward, permitting the snail to move forward on a path of sticky mucus that it secretes beneath it.

Pedal locomotion

Land snail

Muscular foot with sole

Muscle waves

Secreted path sticky mucus

Kangaroo

Hundreds of tube feet under the arms.

Diagram of a tube foot

Starfish

Liquid

Foot extended *Foot contracted*

Peristaltic locomotion

Many animals have no arms or legs, and must use their whole body for movement. This type of movement is called axial locomotion. Snakes are some such animals, and one way they can advance is through what is known as concertina movement, because they squeeze and stretch like a concertina. Extending its head forward, the snake uses the rest of its body as an anchor. Once fully extended, it anchors with its head, pulling up the rest of its body, to start another "step" forward.

Starfish living on the ocean floor move about on hundreds of tiny tube feet carried under each of their "arms." These feet pull the animal along, extending, anchoring and contracting by means of a liquid the starfish pumps into the feet, filling or emptying them. This type of movement is described as peristaltic.

Saltation

Frog

Frogs, kangaroos, rabbits and grasshoppers are just some of the animals that get about by thrusting their hindlegs powerfully, allowing them to jump ahead in bounds, often over considerable distances. This type of locomotion is called saltation.

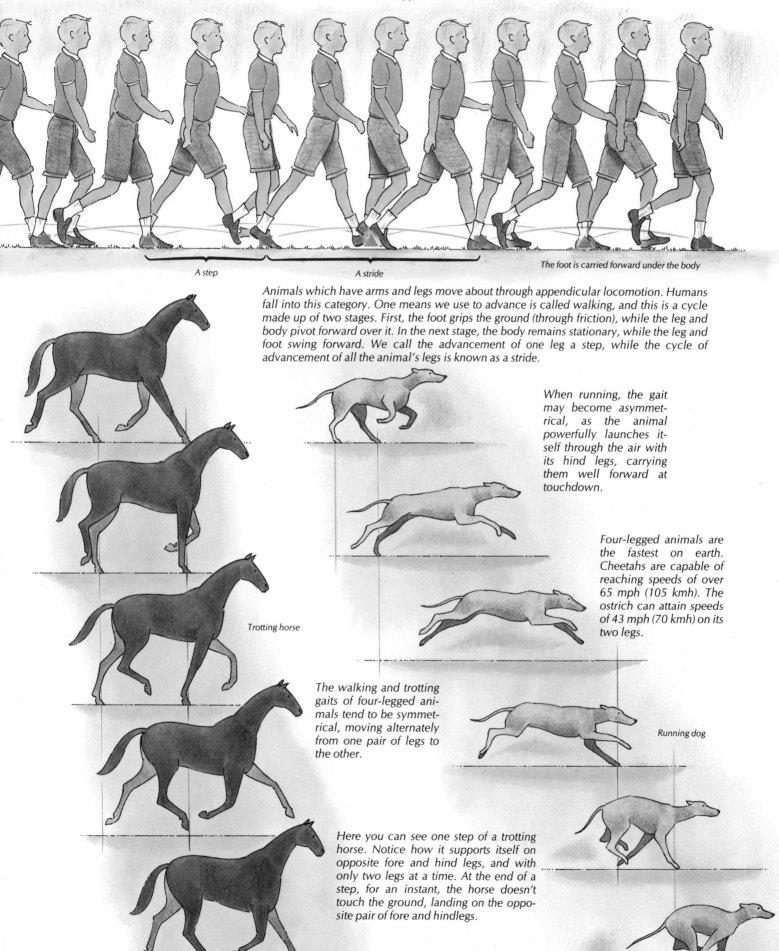

The body pivots forward over the foot

The foot is carried forward under the body

A step

A stride

Animals which have arms and legs move about through appendicular locomotion. Humans fall into this category. One means we use to advance is called walking, and this is a cycle made up of two stages. First, the foot grips the ground (through friction), while the leg and body pivot forward over it. In the next stage, the body remains stationary, while the leg and foot swing forward. We call the advancement of one leg a step, while the cycle of advancement of all the animal's legs is known as a stride.

When running, the gait may become asymmetrical, as the animal powerfully launches itself through the air with its hind legs, carrying them well forward at touchdown.

Four-legged animals are the fastest on earth. Cheetahs are capable of reaching speeds of over 65 mph (105 kmh). The ostrich can attain speeds of 43 mph (70 kmh) on its two legs.

The walking and trotting gaits of four-legged animals tend to be symmetrical, moving alternately from one pair of legs to the other.

Trotting horse

Running dog

Here you can see one step of a trotting horse. Notice how it supports itself on opposite fore and hind legs, and with only two legs at a time. At the end of a step, for an instant, the horse doesn't touch the ground, landing on the opposite pair of fore and hindlegs.

Shaping a hot shoe
on the anvil

Shoeing a horse

Horseshoes were made and fitted at the blacksmith's shop.

People wear shoes to protect their feet, as well as to improve their footing. Similarly, horses are shod with horseshoes, saving their hooves from injury and wear, while giving them a better hold on the ground. Although horseshoes have been made since ancient times, it was not until fairly recently that they were widely fitted.

Roman "hipposandal"

Frankish horseshoe

French horseshoe, 16th century

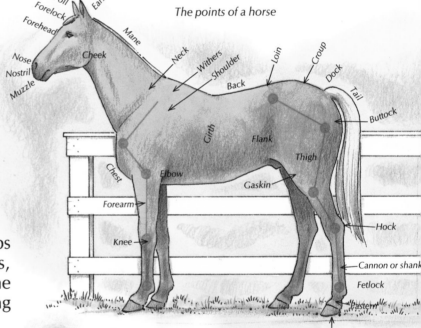

The points of a horse

Horse and Harness

With the exception of the sail on ships and the water wheel on rushing streams, the harnessing of animals is one of the first means found by man of providing nonhuman power to do work.

In ancient times dogs, llamas and oxen were frequently used for pulling sleds and wheeled carts. Later, camels, asses, reindeer and finally horses were trained to be driven, and eventually ridden.

Indeed, until not much more than a century ago, horses still provided the only widespread, rapid source of power for land transportation. Since then, the "iron horse," or railway locomotive, and the automobile, with its "horse-power," have all but replaced the horse on the road. Today, horses are ridden or driven before carriages almost exclusively for pleasure and sport.

The wheel is certainly one of man's most useful inventions, as well as being one of his earliest. Perhaps derived from a rolling log or a tumbling stone, it greatly reduced the friction under any pulled load. It made it possible to transport heavier loads much faster and for greater distances.

Babylonian wheel

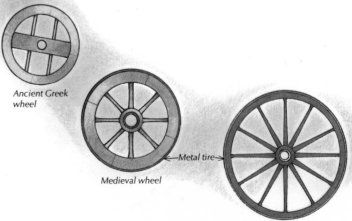

Ancient Greek wheel

Medieval wheel

Metal tire

18th-century wheel

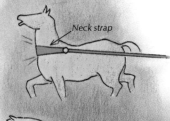

Neck strap

In ancient times harnesses consisted simply of a strap around the horse's neck. The harder the animal pulled, the more it choked.

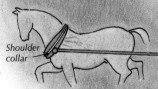

Shoulder collar

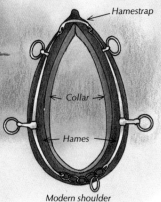

Hamestrap

Collar

Hames

Modern shoulder harness

The modern harness we know today was introduced into Europe from Asia in about 800 A.D. It fits on the horse's shoulders without interfering with its breathing or circulation so the animal can use all its strength for pulling.

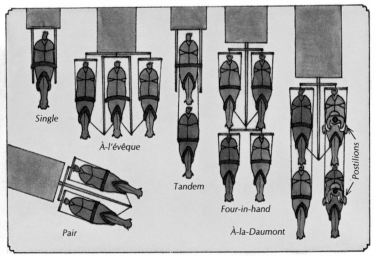

Single

À-l'évêque

Tandem

Four-in-hand

Pair

À-la-Daumont

Postilions

Over the centuries a variety of harnesses were designed for traction by one horse or several. Choice of one arrangement over another depended on the width of the road, speed, cost or the desire for elegance.

English saddle

Crown piece
Throatlatch
Browband
Cheek strap
Noseband
Reins
Bit

Pad
Seat
Flap
Pommel
Cantle

Stirrup leather
Girth
Stirrup

Western Saddle

Cantle
Seat
Pommel

Saddle strings
Flap

Flank strap
Stirrup
Front tie strap

Horses have been ridden for centuries using a variety of saddles. Today, the most popular riding saddle is the lightweight "English" saddle. In America the "Western" saddle was developed to enable cowboys to handle great herds of cattle from horseback. The pommel provided a means of securing the lasso when roping cattle.

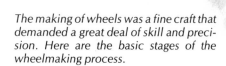

Shaping the parts of the wheel rim, or "felly."

Driving the spokes into the hub

Fitting the fellies to the spokes

A metal tire and its wooden wheel

Fitting hot tire to the wheel

Cooling tire in water

The making of wheels was a fine craft that demanded a great deal of skill and precision. Here are the basic stages of the wheelmaking process.

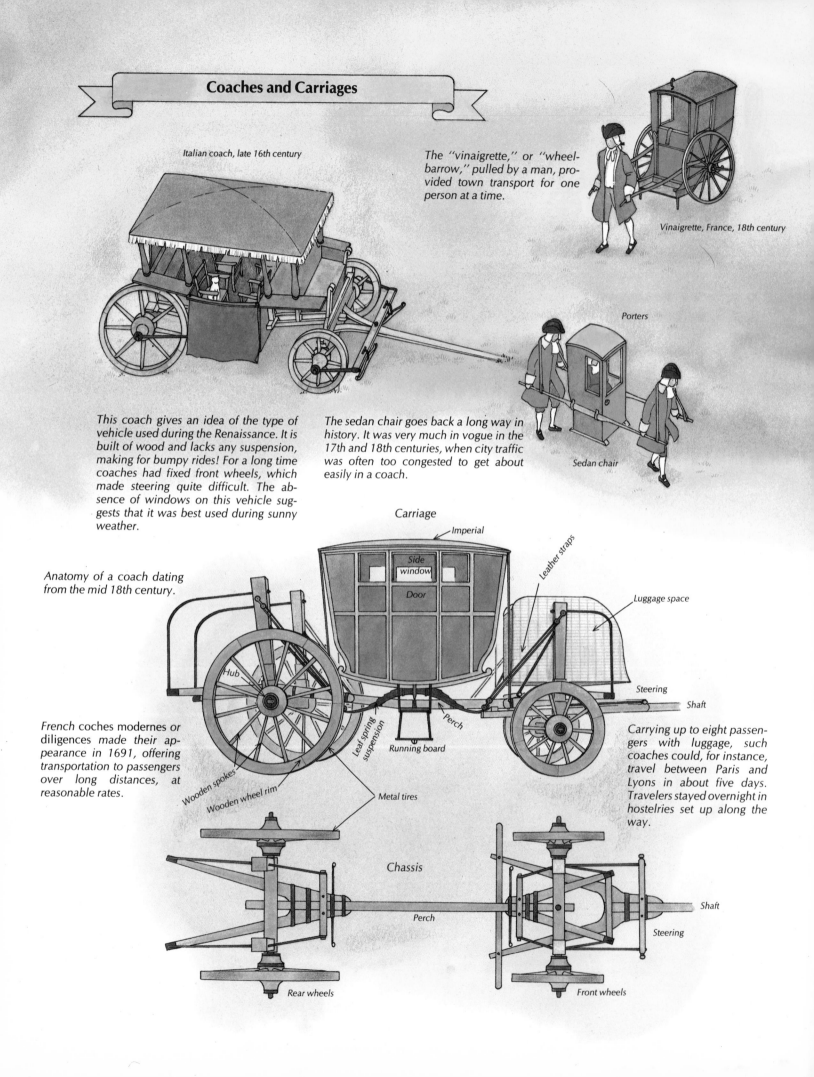

Coaches and Carriages

Italian coach, late 16th century

The "vinaigrette," or "wheelbarrow," pulled by a man, provided town transport for one person at a time.

Vinaigrette, France, 18th century

Porters

Sedan chair

This coach gives an idea of the type of vehicle used during the Renaissance. It is built of wood and lacks any suspension, making for bumpy rides! For a long time coaches had fixed front wheels, which made steering quite difficult. The absence of windows on this vehicle suggests that it was best used during sunny weather.

The sedan chair goes back a long way in history. It was very much in vogue in the 17th and 18th centuries, when city traffic was often too congested to get about easily in a coach.

Carriage

Imperial

Side window

Door

Leather straps

Luggage space

Steering

Shaft

Hub

Leaf spring suspension

Perch

Running board

Anatomy of a coach dating from the mid 18th century.

French coches modernes or diligences made their appearance in 1691, offering transportation to passengers over long distances, at reasonable rates.

Wooden spokes

Wooden wheel rim

Metal tires

Carrying up to eight passengers with luggage, such coaches could, for instance, travel between Paris and Lyons in about five days. Travelers stayed overnight in hostelries set up along the way.

Chassis

Shaft

Perch

Steering

Rear wheels

Front wheels

Conestoga wagon, American Colonies, 18th century

Horse's feed trough

The Conestoga wagon takes its name from the town of Conestoga, Pennsylvania, where it was originally made. The Pioneer settlers used these peculiar boat-shaped wagons to cross the Appalachian mountains, via the Mohawk Trail, Cumberland Road, or Wilderness Road, in search of a new life in the "Wild West."

The post chaise, which dates back to the mid 17th century, was a normal chair placed between two wheels and hitched up to a horse. In its day it was the most rapid and expensive means of transport for a single person. The word "post" in its name refers not to the post office but to the relay stations, where fresh horses could be exchanged for tired ones along the route. The post chaise was driven by a mounted postilion.

Postilion

Door folds forward to enter

Splashboard

Post chaise, France, mid 18th century

Driver

Postman

Shoe, to park without rolling

"Coupé-Landau" postal stagecoach, Switzerland, 1850

Horse-drawn vehicles were built to a variety of designs, to suit different purposes. Here are some classic examples.

Stagecoaches were the forerunners of the intercity buses and trains of today. In many countries the post office organized stagecoach services carrying both passengers and mail. One of the most famous alpine routes was from Lucerne in Switzerland to Milan in Italy, via the St. Gotthard pass. By stagecoach this nonstop trip took 24 hours. Today, by automobile, the same drive is done in a few hours.

Drag

Dogcart

Omnibus

Post chaise

Carrosse

Berlin

Berlin Coupé

Phaeton

Landau

Break

Cabriolet

Machines

We live in a world of machines. Every day we travel in cars, ride in elevators and speak on telephones. Machines help us to do work, or to move around. Almost all machines are made up of moving parts. All moving parts can be defined as one or another very simple element that transforms energy and controls the direction of motion. We call such elements the simple machines. These are the lever, wheel and axle, pulley, wedge, inclined plane and screw. Let's see how machines help us in our everyday life.

A first-class lever

Levers are of three types, called first, second and third-class levers.

First-class levers have the fulcrum placed between the load and the effort. Seesaws are typical first-class levers

A second-class lever

Second-class levers have the load placed between the fulcrum and the effort arm. Wheelbarrows are typical second-class levers.

The wheel and axle is also a first-class lever. Here the load lies on the radius of the axle, the effort is at the crank and the fulcrum lies in the axis of rotation or hub. A pulley wheel is a first-class lever whose load and effort arms are of unequal distance, giving a mechanical advantage thus making it easier to lift heavy weights.

A third-class lever

The third-class lever has the load at one end, the fulcrum at the other, and the effort in between. The driving axle and wheel of an automobile is a typical third-class lever. Such levers require a lot of effort to move the load, since the load travels farther than the effort.

A wedge is a simple machine that magnifies the effort put into it from above, in a sideways direction. Nails and hatchets are well-known wedges. A screw is a wedge wrapped around a cylinder, while the inclined plane, almost too simple to look like a machine, is actually a wedge where the effort is applied directly to the load.

Wedge (inclined plane)

Inclined plane

Load (weight)

Inclined plane (wedge)

Screw (wedge)

The efficiency of a machine is the ratio between the amount of energy put into it, and the amount of energy it puts out. No machine is 100 percent efficient, as all machines use up some of the input energy through friction between moving parts. This energy is lost as heat.

The mechanical advantage of a machine is the ratio between the force put into a machine, and the force it puts out. It is basically the amplification of force.

Electricity generator

Gasoline engine

Drive shaft

Electricity wires

Flow of electrical energy

Drive shaft activates generator: electrical energy

Burning fuel: heat energy

Piston turns drive shaft: mechanical energy

el: chemical ergy

A gasoline engine converts heat energy released by the burning fuel directly into useful mechanical energy.

Electric motor

Rotary saw

Mechanical energy performs work

Belt-driven wheels

Electrical energy turns electromagnets attached to a shaft: mechanical energy

Machines do not create energy, but only transform one kind of energy into another, to perform a particular job. In this drawing, a gasoline engine is transforming heat energy provided by burning fuel, into mechanical energy, which causes the drive shaft to rotate. The rotating drive shaft turns magnet coils inside a generator to transform this energy into electrical energy. Electrical energy can travel over a distance, through wires, to an electric motor. Here the electrical energy turns magnet coils attached to a spinning shaft and is transformed back into mechanical energy. A pair of belt-driven spindles can amplify, or change the direction of movement of this energy to power machinery, in this instance, a rotary saw.

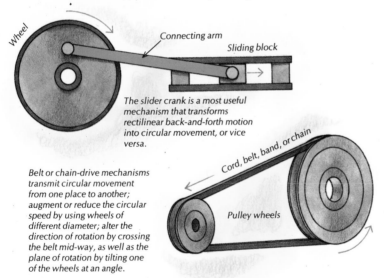

Wheel

Connecting arm

Sliding block

The slider crank is a most useful mechanism that transforms rectilinear back-and-forth motion into circular movement, or vice versa.

Belt or chain-drive mechanisms transmit circular movement from one place to another; augment or reduce the circular speed by using wheels of different diameter; alter the direction of rotation by crossing the belt mid-way, as well as the plane of rotation by tilting one of the wheels at an angle.

Cord, belt, band, or chain

Pulley wheels

Pair of friction discs

The friction clutch transmits circular motion from one shaft to another through simple adhesion of one plate against the other. It allows two shafts to be engaged or disengaged at will.

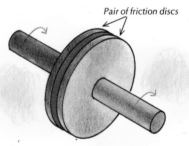

Universal joints of various sorts permit the transmission of circular motion through a variety of different angles.

Universal joint

Mechanisms are simple machines that transmit motion, often modifying its speed and direction. Some of the most common simple mechanisms, which can be found in most machinery, are shown here.

Gears placed in pairs transmit motion and force, into various planes and angles.

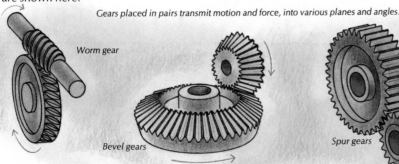

Worm gear

Bevel gears

Spur gears

Rack and pinion gears

Rack and pinion gears change circular, into rectilinear movement.

Worm gears and bevel gears change the direction and speed of rotation.

Spur gears change the speed of rotation and intensity of force.

Anatomy of a Bicycle

Bicycles are among the simplest and best known mechanical vehicles. They comprise a variety of simple machines all of which are easily identifiable. How many of them can you find on your bicycle?

Bicycles were also among the first mechanical vehicles to be developed and their simplicity of design, lightness and easy maintenance still make them one of the most popular means of transport today.

The very first bicycle was invented by Baron Karl Drais von Sauerbronn, which he demonstrated in Paris in 1818. Big, heavy and cumbersome to steer, it was propelled by simply swinging one's legs along the ground, or by coasting downhill. In spite of its clumsiness, it soon became popular, and was known as a "Draisienne" in honor of its inventor.

Baron Drais' "Draisienne"

Spinning top

What keeps a bicycle upright? It is, in fact, the same force that acts on a spinning top, or on a gyroscope, and is called gyroscopic inertia. The rapidly spinning bicycle wheels set up a strong centrifugal force that defies any other . . . even that of gravity. But if you slow the wheels down the force disappears, and you will start to wobble. Similarly, a quickly spinning top stands up by itself, but as it slows down, it wobbles and finally falls over.

The "dérailleur" gear-change mechanism operates through a small lever and cable, which acts on a parallelogram device at the rear hub. This moves sprockets, which guide the roller chain from side to side, allowing the chain to engage with a number of toothed driving sprockets attached to the rear wheel hub. Most rear wheel dérailleurs carry five gear sprockets. The bigger sprockets are the low gears, while the smaller ones are the high gears. Very often, the driving sprocket carries a second, smaller one. Five speeds at the rear, and two up front give the rider ten gear ratios to choose from.

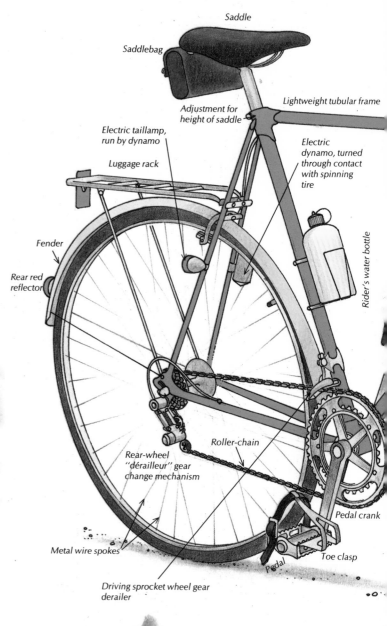

Saddle

Saddlebag

Lightweight tubular frame

Adjustment for height of saddle

Electric taillamp, run by dynamo

Electric dynamo, turned through contact with spinning tire

Luggage rack

Rider's water bottle

Fender

Rear red reflector

Roller-chain

Rear-wheel "dérailleur" gear change mechanism

Pedal crank

Metal wire spokes

Pedal

Toe clasp

Driving sprocket wheel gear derailer

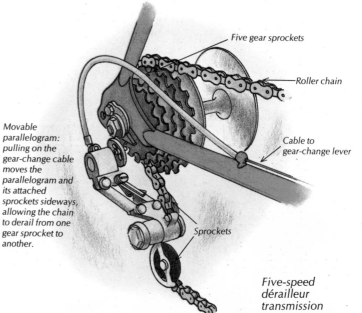

Five gear sprockets

Roller chain

Movable parallelogram: pulling on the gear-change cable moves the parallelogram and its attached sprockets sideways, allowing the chain to derail from one gear sprocket to another.

Cable to gear-change lever

Sprockets

Five-speed dérailleur transmission

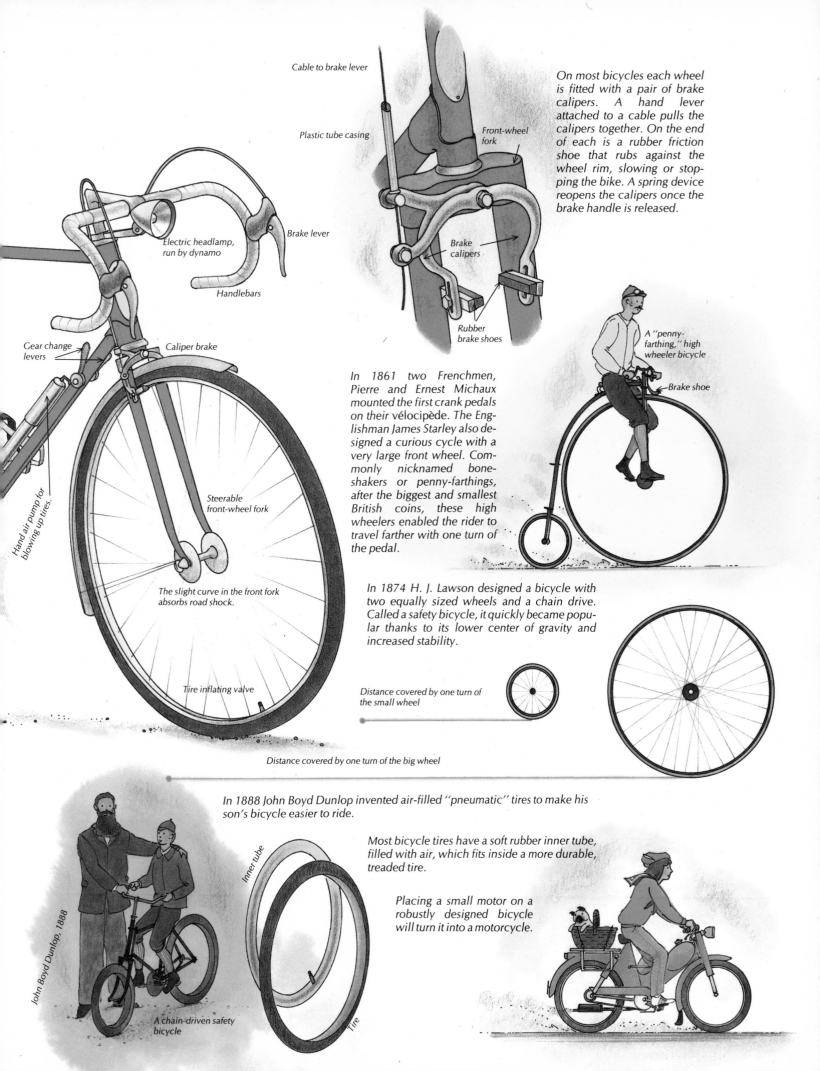

Cable to brake lever

Plastic tube casing

Front-wheel fork

On most bicycles each wheel is fitted with a pair of brake calipers. A hand lever attached to a cable pulls the calipers together. On the end of each is a rubber friction shoe that rubs against the wheel rim, slowing or stopping the bike. A spring device reopens the calipers once the brake handle is released.

Brake calipers

Rubber brake shoes

Electric headlamp, run by dynamo

Brake lever

Handlebars

Gear change levers

Caliper brake

Hand air pump for blowing up tires.

Steerable front-wheel fork

The slight curve in the front fork absorbs road shock.

Tire inflating valve

A "penny-farthing," high wheeler bicycle

Brake shoe

In 1861 two Frenchmen, Pierre and Ernest Michaux mounted the first crank pedals on their vélocipède. The Englishman James Starley also designed a curious cycle with a very large front wheel. Commonly nicknamed boneshakers or penny-farthings, after the biggest and smallest British coins, these high wheelers enabled the rider to travel farther with one turn of the pedal.

In 1874 H. J. Lawson designed a bicycle with two equally sized wheels and a chain drive. Called a safety bicycle, it quickly became popular thanks to its lower center of gravity and increased stability.

Distance covered by one turn of the small wheel

Distance covered by one turn of the big wheel

In 1888 John Boyd Dunlop invented air-filled "pneumatic" tires to make his son's bicycle easier to ride.

Most bicycle tires have a soft rubber inner tube, filled with air, which fits inside a more durable, treaded tire.

Inner tube

Placing a small motor on a robustly designed bicycle will turn it into a motorcycle.

John Boyd Dunlop, 1888

A chain-driven safety bicycle

Tire

Baron Drais von Sauerbronn's "Draisienne," Germany, 1817

Nicéphore Niepce made this steerable vélocifère in 1818.

Steerable front wheel

Steerable front wheel

The German Baron Drais von Sauerbronn patented his steerable "Draisienne" in 1817. In 1818, when he first presented his invention to the public in Paris, he was met with ridicule. Today he is considered the father of the bicycle.

Comte de Sivrac's célerifère, France, 1791

Niepce vélocifère, France, 1818

The Comte de Sivrac is believed to be the inventor of the very first "pedestrian hobby-horse," which he pushed about Paris with his feet.

A number of unusual designs for cycles appeared in the second half of the 19th century. Among these was the "dicycle," patented by E. C. T. Otto between 1879 and 1881. Steering was controlled by slackening one drive belt, thus permitting the wheels to turn at different speeds.

Otto "dicycle," Great Britain, 1880

Drive belt, slackened for steering

Anatomy of a motorcycle

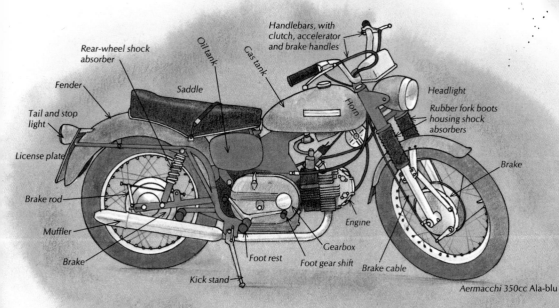

Handlebars, with clutch, accelerator and brake handles

Rear-wheel shock absorber

Oil tank

Gas tank

Fender

Saddle

Horn

Headlight

Tail and stop light

Rubber fork boots housing shock absorbers

License plate

Brake

Brake rod

Muffler

Engine

Brake

Gearbox

Foot rest

Foot gear shift

Brake cable

Kick stand

Aermacchi 350cc Ala-blu

Smaller-engined scooters and lightweight motorbikes are popular around the world today.

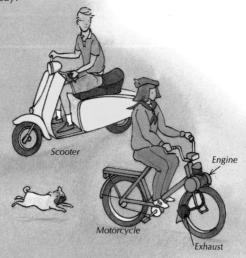

Scooter

Engine

Motorcycle

Exhaust

In 1885 Gottlieb Daimler built this motorized bicycle, which he called a "riding car." It is a forerunner of the motorcycle.

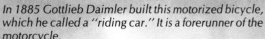

Gottlieb Daimler's "riding-car," Germany, 1885

Michaux gas-powered vélocipède, France, 1869

Pierre and Ernest Michaux fitted a small gasoline engine to one of their vélocipèdes in 1869, giving them credit for making the first motorcycle.

Macmillan's push pedal hobby-horse, Great Britain, 1839

Push pedal

A Scottish blacksmith, Kirkpatrick Macmillan, built the first bicycle powered by pedals, which the rider pushed back and forth with his feet.

Brake

Crank pedals

Michaux vélocipède, France, 1860s

The coachbuilder Pierre Michaux and his son Ernest were the first to attach crank pedals to the wheel of a bicycle, which they successfully rode in Paris in 1861. The Michaux family began manufacturing vélocipèdes, which became very popular.

In 1870 the Englishman James Starley, who was manufacturing Michaux vélocipèdes in England, set about to improve the vehicle. He reduced their weight, and enlarged the front wheel, enabling faster speeds to be attained.

Starley bicycle, Great Britain, 1872

Harry John Lawson's "bicyclette," Great Britain, 1879

Chain drive

H. J. Lawson made the first chain-driven bicycle, making the wheels smaller, and thus putting the rider closer to the ground. Lawson called his cycle a bicyclette, but it soon became known as the safety bicycle, while high wheelers became ordinaries. Safeties made cycling easier for everybody.

Racing high wheeler, 1884

High wheelers were often raced by dashing young men. The diameter of the driving wheel was limited only by the length of the rider's legs.

Pneumatic tires

John Boyd Dunlop's pneumatic tires on a safety bicycle, Great Britain, 1888

The Scotsman John Boyd Dunlop, looking for a way to soften the ride on his son's bicycle, fitted air-filled tires to it. This not only made riding softer, but faster. Today, the invention of pneumatic tires is attributed to Dunlop.

Lightweight racing bicycle (with no brakes) following a quintuplet team of trainers, late 19th century.

Bicycle races, either outdoors on the road, or indoors on special oval tracks, quickly became popular. Champions on lightweight machines trained for races by pacing themselves behind a powerful team of trainers.

A major development in bicycle design came in 1962, when the Englishman Alexander Moulton invented a bicycle with a very low center of gravity and excellent suspension.

Luggage rack

Shock absorber

Flexible suspension

Moulton bicycle, Great Britain, 1962

Steam Power

In the kitchen you will certainly have noticed how a loosely-placed kettle lid rattles about once the water begins to boil. What you are in fact looking at is a simple steam engine! The rattling top, pushed about by the expanding steam inside, demonstrates, in a modest way, the wonderful power of steam. Properly harnessed, steam can be put to work to run large machines, such as locomotives. Let's have a look at what steam is, and how it can be put to work.

According to temperature, water can change from a liquid into either a solid or a gas. For instance, in winter a pond may freeze, while on a hot summer day a haze may develop above its surface. This haze is in fact evaporated water, or steam. When water changes its state it also changes its volume. A given amount of water will occupy slightly more space as ice, whereas, if boiled entirely into steam – saturated steam – its volume will be 1,670 times as big. If this expanding steam is tightly confined it will create the pressure needed to lift the kettle lid or even drive the pistons of a great steam locomotive.

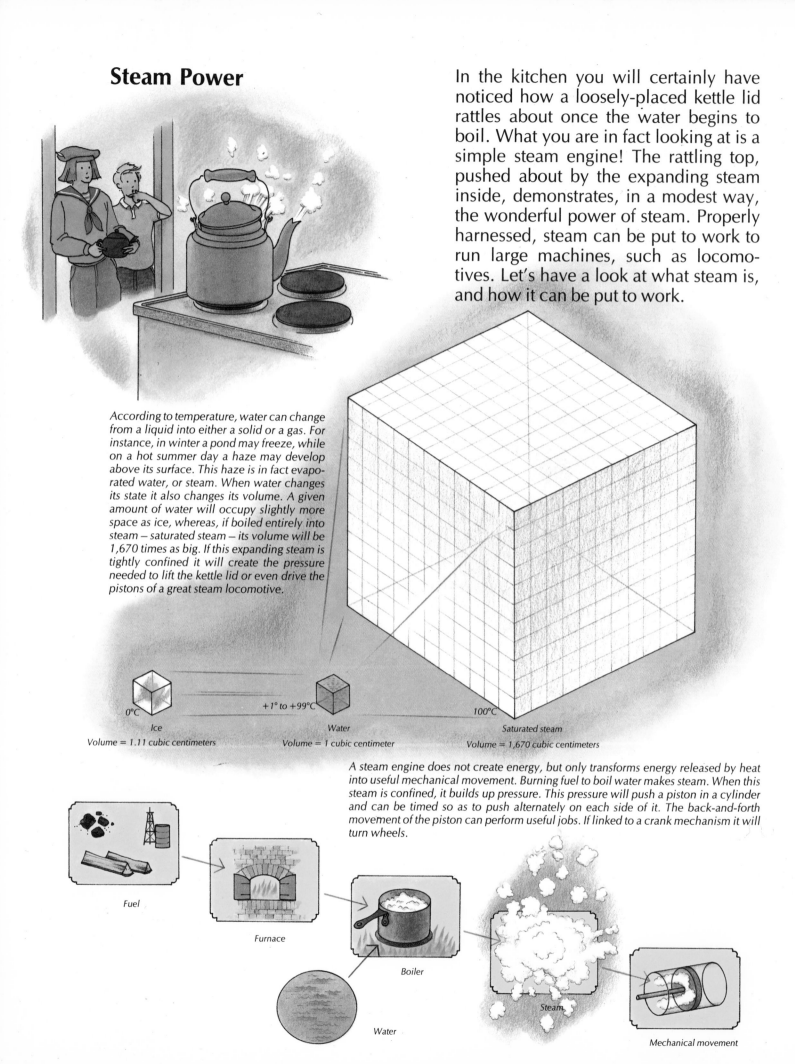

0°C
Ice
Volume = 1.11 cubic centimeters

+1° to +99°C
Water
Volume = 1 cubic centimeter

100°C
Saturated steam
Volume = 1,670 cubic centimeters

A steam engine does not create energy, but only transforms energy released by heat into useful mechanical movement. Burning fuel to boil water makes steam. When this steam is confined, it builds up pressure. This pressure will push a piston in a cylinder and can be timed so as to push alternately on each side of it. The back-and-forth movement of the piston can perform useful jobs. If linked to a crank mechanism it will turn wheels.

Fuel

Furnace

Boiler

Water

Steam

Mechanical movement

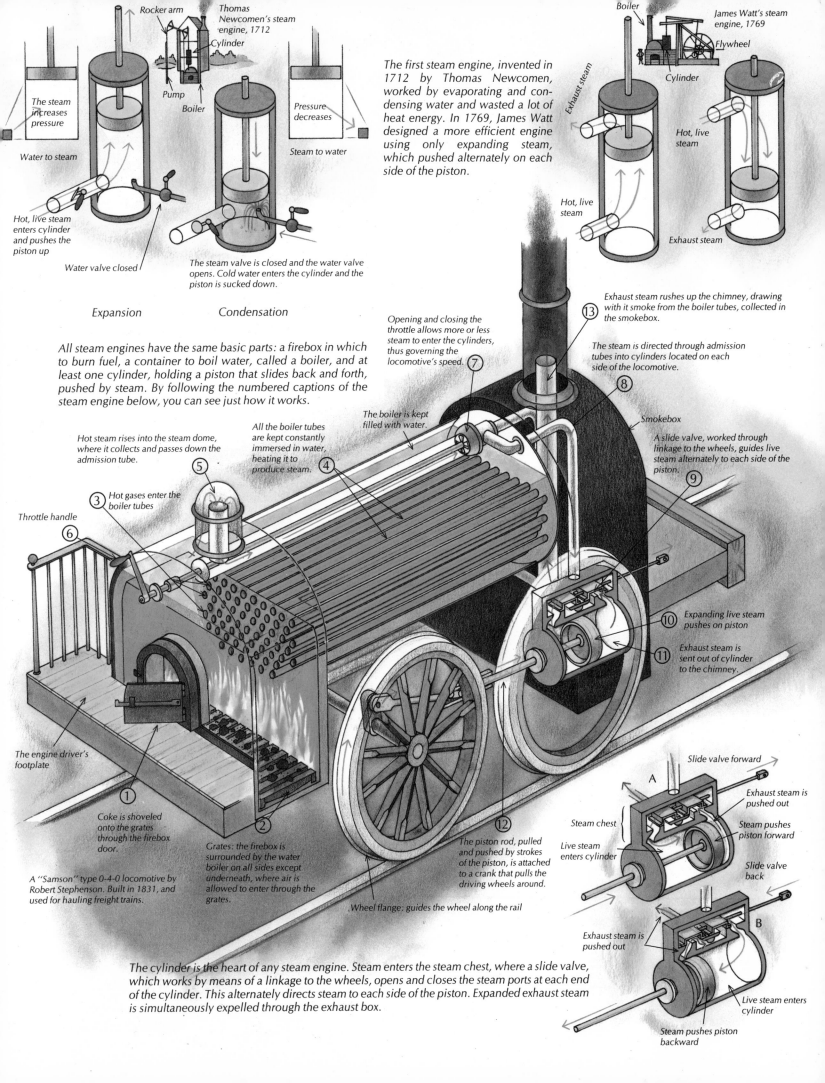

Rocker arm

Thomas Newcomen's steam engine, 1712

Cylinder

Pump

Boiler

The steam increases pressure

Pressure decreases

Water to steam

Steam to water

Hot, live steam enters cylinder and pushes the piston up

Water valve closed

The steam valve is closed and the water valve opens. Cold water enters the cylinder and the piston is sucked down.

Expansion

Condensation

Boiler

James Watt's steam engine, 1769

Flywheel

Cylinder

Exhaust steam

Hot, live steam

Hot, live steam

Exhaust steam

The first steam engine, invented in 1712 by Thomas Newcomen, worked by evaporating and condensing water and wasted a lot of heat energy. In 1769, James Watt designed a more efficient engine using only expanding steam, which pushed alternately on each side of the piston.

All steam engines have the same basic parts: a firebox in which to burn fuel, a container to boil water, called a boiler, and at least one cylinder, holding a piston that slides back and forth, pushed by steam. By following the numbered captions of the steam engine below, you can see just how it works.

Opening and closing the throttle allows more or less steam to enter the cylinders, thus governing the locomotive's speed.

Exhaust steam rushes up the chimney, drawing with it smoke from the boiler tubes, collected in the smokebox.

The steam is directed through admission tubes into cylinders located on each side of the locomotive.

Hot steam rises into the steam dome, where it collects and passes down the admission tube.

All the boiler tubes are kept constantly immersed in water, heating it to produce steam.

The boiler is kept filled with water.

Smokebox

A slide valve, worked through linkage to the wheels, guides live steam alternately to each side of the piston.

Throttle handle

Hot gases enter the boiler tubes

Expanding live steam pushes on piston

Exhaust steam is sent out of cylinder to the chimney.

The engine driver's footplate

Coke is shoveled onto the grates through the firebox door.

A ''Samson'' type 0-4-0 locomotive by Robert Stephenson. Built in 1831, and used for hauling freight trains.

Grates: the firebox is surrounded by the water boiler on all sides except underneath, where air is allowed to enter through the grates.

The piston rod, pulled and pushed by strokes of the piston, is attached to a crank that pulls the driving wheels around.

Wheel flange: guides the wheel along the rail

Slide valve forward

Exhaust steam is pushed out

Steam chest

Steam pushes piston forward

Live steam enters cylinder

Slide valve back

Exhaust steam is pushed out

Live steam enters cylinder

Steam pushes piston backward

The cylinder is the heart of any steam engine. Steam enters the steam chest, where a slide valve, which works by means of a linkage to the wheels, opens and closes the steam ports at each end of the cylinder. This alternately directs steam to each side of the piston. Expanded exhaust steam is simultaneously expelled through the exhaust box.

Pressure gauge for heating system in carriages

Cab lamp

Ordinary whistle

Boiler water level gauges

Speedometer

Boiler steam pressure gauge

Emergency whistle

Ordinary whistle

Sanding control

Air brake pressure gauge

Reversing wheel, to set the locomotive into backward motion

Fireman's seat

Throttle handle

Door to firebox

Engineer's seat

The dozens of controls inside the cab of a steam locomotive required skill, experience and the constant attention of both the engineer and the fireman. Some of the most important controls are shown here in this illustration of the cab of an English locomotive.

This "Baltic" compound express locomotive was built in France in 1911. She was one of the biggest and heaviest steam locomotives in Europe at that time, weighing 102 tons, with driving wheels of 6 ft. 8¼in. (2.04 meters) in diameter.

Steam can be "superheated," giving it more expanding force by sending it back through superheating tubes located within the boiler tubes.

Sand dome: sand, sprinkled in front of the driving wheels, increases adhesion on wet rails or inclines.

Safety valve: this releases steam pressure in the boiler.

Steam rises and is collected in the dome.

Throttle

Water level: the boiler tubes must always be submerged.

Sand tubes

Engineer's cab

Firebox door

Air is heated up in the firebox, passes through the boiler tubes and brings the water to boiling point.

Brick shield

Fuel is burned on the grate.

31102

Connecting rod

Piston rod

Bogie

Trailing wheels

Steam injectors shoot water from the tender into the boiler.

Wheel flange

Balancing counterweight helps rotation

Driving wheels

Brake shoe, operated by compressed air

Wheel arrangements depended on the type of locomotive and were described by the number of wheels or axles. Generally, goods locomotives had small driving wheels for maximum adhesion, and expresses had large ones for extra speed. Here are some famous arrangements which became classics.

Wheel count

Axle count

2-2-0 American 4-4-0

0-3-0 Six wheel switcher 0-6-0

1-3-1 Prairie 2-6-2

2-2-1 Atlantic 4-4-2

1-3-0 Mogul 2-6-0

2-3-0 Ten wheeler 4-6-0

Steam Locomotives

There is no more exciting sight than that of a steam locomotive in action. With its puffing smoke and hissing steam it almost seems to be alive. Even today, long after electric and diesel locomotives have replaced them, no one would dispute their fascination and beauty. Let's take a look inside and try and understand why.

Water tank

A steam locomotive burns either coal, wood, or oil to heat water to make steam. All the fuel and water had to be carried with the locomotive, so often a special tender was pulled along behind. Large locomotives consumed tremendous amounts of water, so frequent stops to take on water were necessary on every trip.

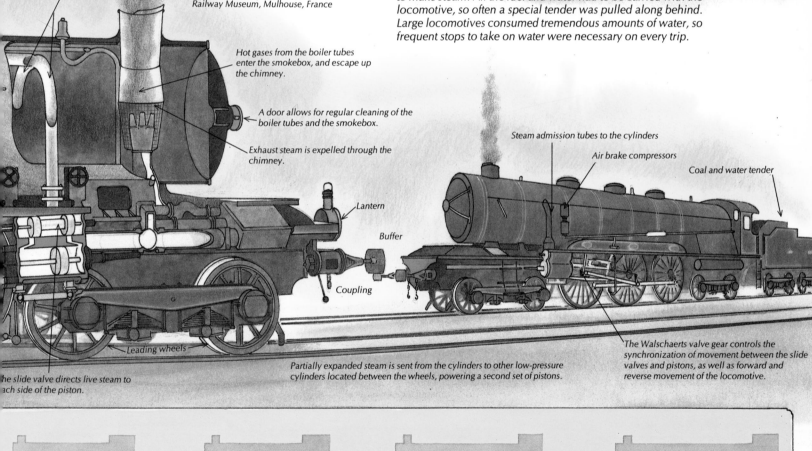

Steam is sent through admission tubes to the cylinders.

Drawn from an exhibit in the National Railway Museum, Mulhouse, France

Hot gases from the boiler tubes enter the smokebox, and escape up the chimney.

A door allows for regular cleaning of the boiler tubes and the smokebox.

Exhaust steam is expelled through the chimney.

Lantern

Buffer

Coupling

Leading wheels

he slide valve directs live steam to ach side of the piston.

Partially expanded steam is sent from the cylinders to other low-pressure cylinders located between the wheels, powering a second set of pistons.

Steam admission tubes to the cylinders

Air brake compressors

Coal and water tender

The Walschaerts valve gear controls the synchronization of movement between the slide valves and pistons, as well as forward and reverse movement of the locomotive.

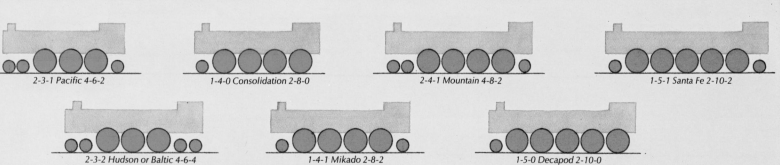

2-3-1 Pacific 4-6-2

1-4-0 Consolidation 2-8-0

2-4-1 Mountain 4-8-2

1-5-1 Santa Fe 2-10-2

2-3-2 Hudson or Baltic 4-6-4

1-4-1 Mikado 2-8-2

1-5-0 Decapod 2-10-0

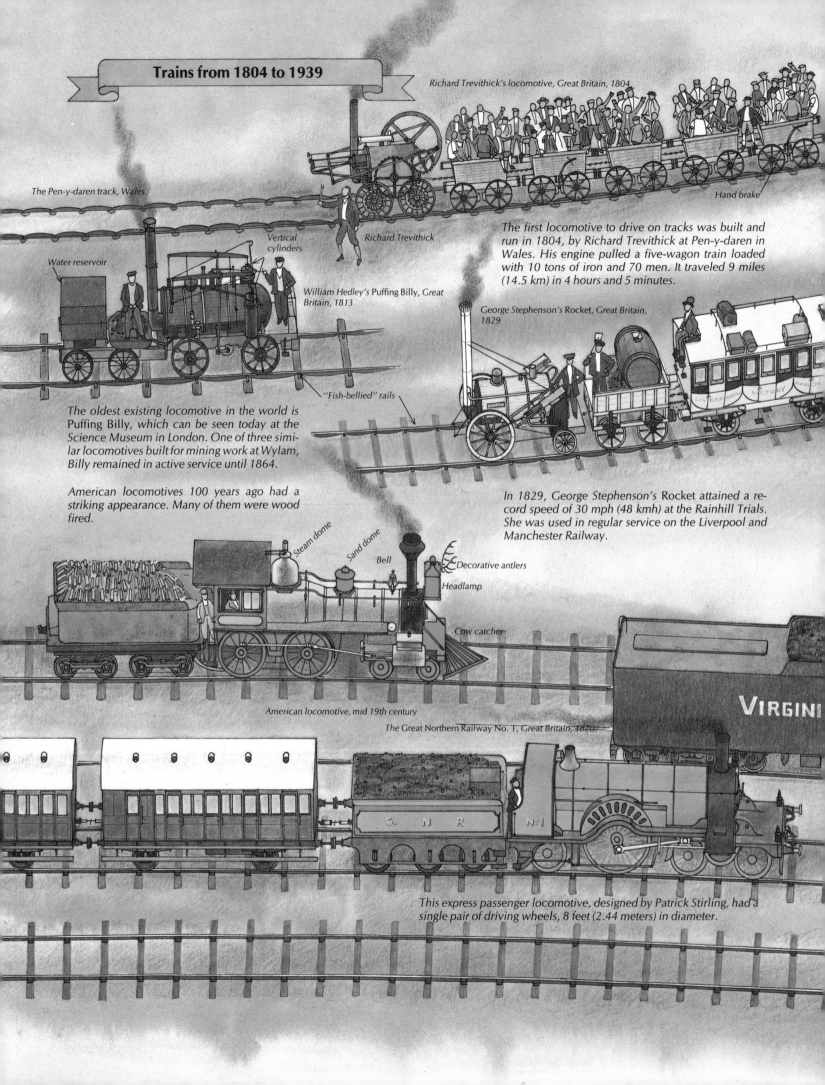

Trains from 1804 to 1939

Richard Trevithick's locomotive, Great Britain, 1804

The Pen-y-daren track, Wales.

Hand brake

Richard Trevithick

Water reservoir

Vertical cylinders

William Hedley's Puffing Billy, Great Britain, 1813

"Fish-bellied" rails

The first locomotive to drive on tracks was built and run in 1804, by Richard Trevithick at Pen-y-daren in Wales. His engine pulled a five-wagon train loaded with 10 tons of iron and 70 men. It traveled 9 miles (14.5 km) in 4 hours and 5 minutes.

George Stephenson's Rocket, Great Britain, 1829

The oldest existing locomotive in the world is Puffing Billy, which can be seen today at the Science Museum in London. One of three similar locomotives built for mining work at Wylam, Billy remained in active service until 1864.

American locomotives 100 years ago had a striking appearance. Many of them were wood fired.

In 1829, George Stephenson's Rocket attained a record speed of 30 mph (48 kmh) at the Rainhill Trials. She was used in regular service on the Liverpool and Manchester Railway.

Steam dome

Sand dome

Bell

Decorative antlers

Headlamp

Cow catcher

American locomotive, mid 19th century

The Great Northern Railway No. 1, Great Britain, 1870

VIRGINI

G N R   N°1

This express passenger locomotive, designed by Patrick Stirling, had a single pair of driving wheels, 8 feet (2.44 meters) in diameter.

Horse drawn rail coach Hannibal, Austria, 1841

The first commercial railway in continental Europe opened in 1832 and ran from Budweis to Linz, in Austria. The line was operated solely with harnessed horses.

Second class carriage, mid 19th century and a second class carriage from the mid 20th century.

Compartment

Luggage rack

Ventilator

Heaters

Toilet

Sprung suspension

Early railway carriages resembled horse drawn coaches. But the small, dark, unsprung wagons of the past have made way for the spacious, airy and smooth carriages of today, equipped with heating and air conditioning, making modern rail travel perhaps the most comfortable mode of transportation available.

This giant locomotive, built for the Virginian Railroad by the Chesapeake & Ohio Railroad weighed some 724,500 lbs (328,198 kilos) and developed 7000 drawbar horsepower. She is typical of the powerful locomotives used to haul long trains of coal or iron ore. No speedsters, these giants could only do about 35 mph (56 kmh).

2-6-6-6 Mallet single expansion locomotive, USA, 1930s

900

The first streamlined trains to operate in Great Britain were the Silver Link trains, entering service in 1935, and traveling between London and Newcastle at speeds of 75 to 90 mph (120 to 145 kmh).

2512

L N E R

London & North Eastern Railway (LNER) streamlined "Pacific" locomotive, named Silver Fox, Great Britain, late 1930s

Magic in a Magnet, a Wizard in a Wire

Electricity, one of our most versatile, adaptable, efficient, powerful, and most widely used energy sources, is also one of the most difficult to understand.

In our everyday life, just about every machine we use gets its power from electricity. In land transportation, its best application has been to electric locomotives. But before we look at these, let's try to understand the basic principles of electric power.

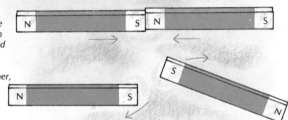

Magnets have a strange, invisible force enabling them to pick up bits of metal without hooks, or glue. Two bar magnets, placed one way, will stick to each other, while placed in another, push apart.

All magnets have two poles, which we call North and South. Unlike magnetic poles attract one another, while like poles repel.

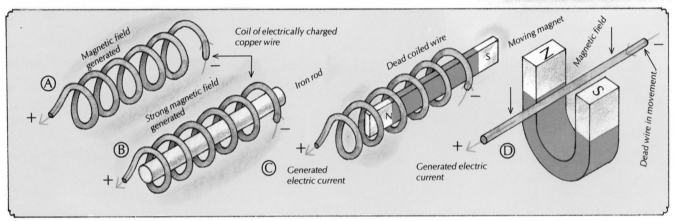

A — Magnetic field generated — Coil of electrically charged copper wire

B — Strong magnetic field generated — Iron rod

C — Dead coiled wire — Generated electric current

D — Moving magnet — Magnetic field — Generated electric current — Dead wire in movement

Magnetism and electricity are closely related. In A, an electric current passing through a piece of coiled wire will cause a magnetic field to be formed around it. Placing a rod of iron inside the coil, as in B, will strengthen this magnetic field considerably. (This is an electromagnet.) In C, an electric current can be generated in a dead coil of wire, by moving a magnet through it. Similarly, a piece of dead wire,

moved through a magnetic field, will become charged with electric current, D. An electric current will only be made as long as there is the proper movement between the wire, and the magnetic field. This is how electricity is generated in big power plants. The phenomenon by which a magnetic field generates electricity, and vice versa, is called electromagnetic induction.

What is electric current?

Simplified diagram of an atom:

...of a conductor. The electron has a loose orbit.

...of an insulator. The electron has a tight orbit.

You have doubtlessly already seen a diagram of an atom. A large mass in the center is called the nucleus, and this is orbited by a number of smaller electrons. In some materials, like silver, iron, or copper, the electrons' orbits are very loose. Under the influence of magnetism, these electrons can actually be tugged out of their orbit, and drift to another atom. This drift of electrons from one atom to the next is electric current. Materials which allow such drift are called conductors.

Atoms of a conductor with their loose orbiting electrons

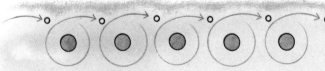

Influenced by a magnetic field, drifting electrons make an electric current.

Electric current can, of course, also be generated through chemical reactions, which is what happens in batteries.

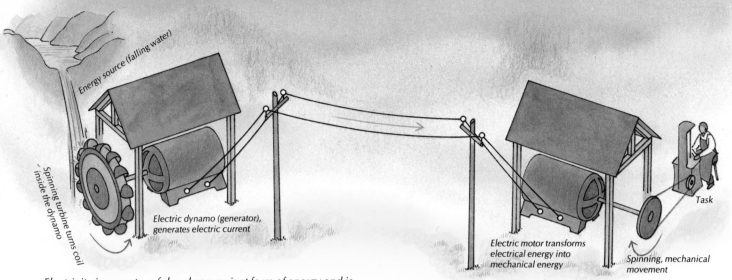

Spinning turbine turns coil inside the dynamo

Energy source (falling water)

Electric dynamo (generator), generates electric current

Electric motor transforms electrical energy into mechanical energy

Spinning, mechanical movement

Task

Electricity is a most useful and convenient form of energy and is highly efficient, losing little of its power through friction or heat. Using a turbine, it can be generated from a variety of energy sources, be it falling water, or expanding steam. The current can

then be transported over long distances by wires to an electric motor, which changes the current back into a mechanical spinning movement, ready to do any job.

Electric generator

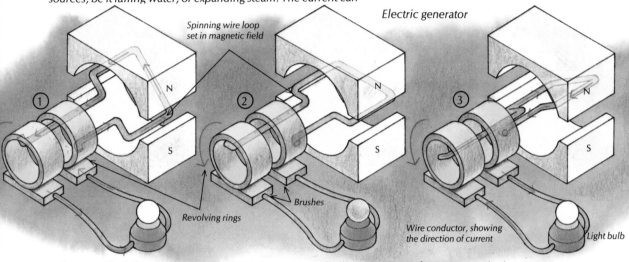

Spinning wire loop set in magnetic field

① N S

② N S   Brushes

Revolving rings

③ N S

Wire conductor, showing the direction of current

Light bulb

Alternating current is the type that we use in our homes. The electric current passing through our appliances and lights actually changes direction dozens of times in one second – too fast for us to notice. In real generators, a number of powerful electromagnets are used, and the wire loop is actually a number of thick, wire coils.

In this simplified diagram, we can see how electricity is generated in an "alternating current" generator. A wire loop, whose ends are attached to a pair of rotating metal rings, is placed inside a magnetic field. When the loop is set in motion, by an outside force (a turbine), an electric current is generated in it. Brushes in contact with the rings, pick up the current, which is sent through wires to the light

bulb (or an electric motor). In 1, the loop in movement cuts the lines of magnetic force, and current is generated in one direction. When the loop is parallel to the magnetic field, as in 2, the magnetic lines of force are not being cut, so no current is generated. As the loop continues its turn, in 3, the lines of force are cut again, but the current has reversed its direction.

An electric motor works like a generator, but the effects are reversed. Using a brush, electric current is picked up from wires by a revolving "commutator," which sends it through a loop, called the armature, placed in a magnetic field. By means of another brush, the current then passes into a series of wires wound around a pair of electromagnets, called the winding, causing the magnets to work, pulling and pushing on the spinning armature. The armature, of course, is also charged, but the split commutator, as it turns, constantly changes the armature's polarity, so that it always spins in the same direction. A spinning shaft attached to the armature can be hooked up to do any job.

Electric motor

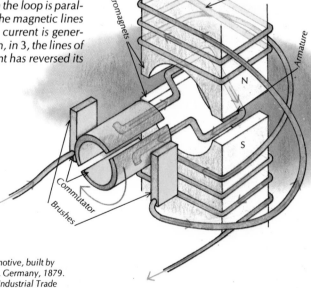

Electromagnets

Winding

Armature

N

S

Commutator

Brushes

First electric locomotive, built by Siemens & Halske, Germany, 1879. (Run at the Berlin Industrial Trade Exhibition, 1879.)

The first electric railway locomotive was designed as an attraction at the Berlin Industrial Trade Exhibition of 1879. It pulled three carriages holding six persons each. Running along a circular track 300 meters long, it had a top speed of some 7 kmh (4 mph).

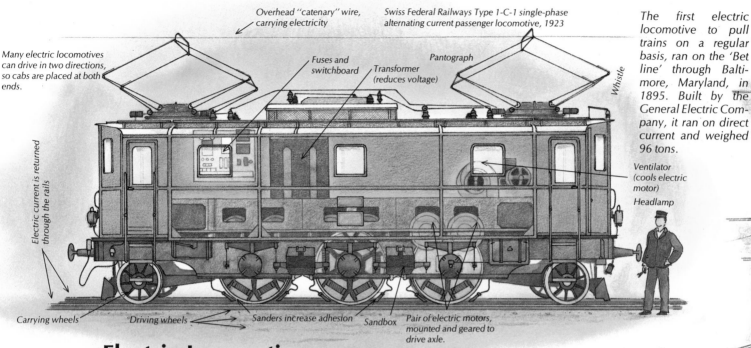

Overhead "catenary" wire, carrying electricity

Swiss Federal Railways Type 1-C-1 single-phase alternating current passenger locomotive, 1923

Fuses and switchboard

Transformer (reduces voltage)

Pantograph

Whistle

Many electric locomotives can drive in two directions, so cabs are placed at both ends.

Electric current is returned through the rails

The first electric locomotive to pull trains on a regular basis, ran on the 'Bet line' through Balti- more, Maryland, in 1895. Built by the General Electric Com- pany, it ran on direct current and weighed 96 tons.

Ventilator (cools electric motor)

Headlamp

Carrying wheels

Driving wheels

Sanders increase adhesion

Sandbox

Pair of electric motors, mounted and geared to drive axle

Electric Locomotives

Most trains around the world today are pulled by electric locomotives. This is because they are powerful, clean and dependable. Electric locomotives re- ceive electricity to drive their motors either through overhead wires, or from a third electrified rail near the track. Diesel-electric locomotives make their own electricity. Diesel engines housed inside turn dynamos, which make elec- tricity to drive the motors.

Between 1904 and 1909, the Oerlikon engineering company successfully tested two electric locomotives on the Seebach– Wettingen line, in Switzerland. Eva had a maximum speed of 37 mph (60 kmh) and was pow- ered by single-phase alternat- ing current.

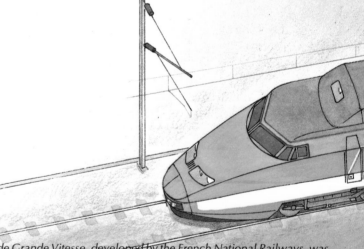

The TGV or Train de Grande Vitesse, developed by the French National Railways, was put into regular service in 1981 and broke the railway speed record, traveling at 236 mph (380 kmh).

Japan built a new railway between Tokyo and Osaka, called the New Tokaido Line (NTL). Opened in 1964, its intercity trains travel up to 155 mph (250 kmh).

Speedometer, clock, and tachygraph

Timetable and reading lamp

Voltmeters and ampmeters

Auxiliary switches

Brake handles

Control panel lock

Main manipulator (accelerator handle)

"Deadman" vigilance pedal

The driving cab of a modern electric locomotive contrasts sharply with that of a steam locomotive. It is of neat, clean and simple design and its large windshield provides the engineer with a good view of the track and signals ahead. As a safety measure, the engineer must always keep the vigilance pedal depressed, otherwise the locomotive will automatically be stopped by its brakes.

Electric locomotive "No. 1," Baltimore & Ohio Railroad, USA, 1895

Electric locomotive, Burgdorf-Thun Railway, Switzerland, 1899

The Brown–Boveri Company built this electric locomotive, the first in regular operation in Europe. She was capable of 22 mph (36 kmh) with passenger trains and of 12 mph (18 kmh) with freight.

The first electric underground railway began operation in London, in 1890.

Crompton electric locomotive and Padded cell passenger car, City & South London Railway, Great Britain, 1900.

Eva Ce 4/4 Type, Seebach-Wettingen Railway, Switzerland, 1904

Crocodile Ce 6/8 II Type freight locomotive, Switzerland, 1920

The Swiss Federal Railways ran powerful locomotives like this one on the steep St. Gotthard line. Known as "Crocodiles," they weighed 126 tons and had a top speed of 46 mph (75 kmh).

TGV, France, 1981

NTL train, Japan, 1964

Electric locomotives, like steam locomotives, are designated by letters and numbers indicating pairs of driving wheels (A, B, C, D) and pairs of carrying wheels (1, 2, 3, 4). Here are some typical examples.

B-B   Connecting rod   C

C-C   1-C-1   2-D-2

Proceed with Caution

Many trains use the same line of track, often in opposite directions. It is therefore very important to have a complex system of signals to prevent accidents. Nowadays, these systems are entirely automatic and work electronically, making accidents virtually impossible.

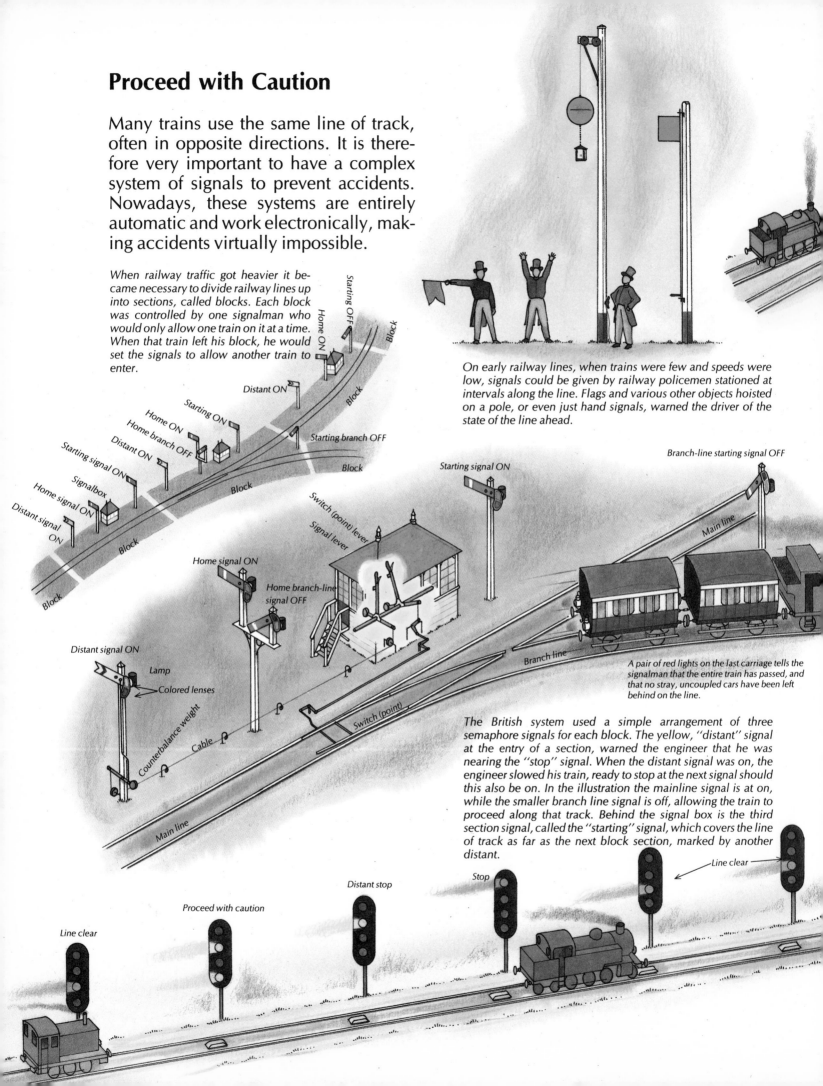

When railway traffic got heavier it became necessary to divide railway lines up into sections, called blocks. Each block was controlled by one signalman who would only allow one train on it at a time. When that train left his block, he would set the signals to allow another train to enter.

On early railway lines, when trains were few and speeds were low, signals could be given by railway policemen stationed at intervals along the line. Flags and various other objects hoisted on a pole, or even just hand signals, warned the driver of the state of the line ahead.

A pair of red lights on the last carriage tells the signalman that the entire train has passed, and that no stray, uncoupled cars have been left behind on the line.

The British system used a simple arrangement of three semaphore signals for each block. The yellow, "distant" signal at the entry of a section, warned the engineer that he was nearing the "stop" signal. When the distant signal was on, the engineer slowed his train, ready to stop at the next signal should this also be on. In the illustration the mainline signal is at on, while the smaller branch line signal is off, allowing the train to proceed along that track. Behind the signal box is the third section signal, called the "starting" signal, which covers the line of track as far as the next block section, marked by another distant.

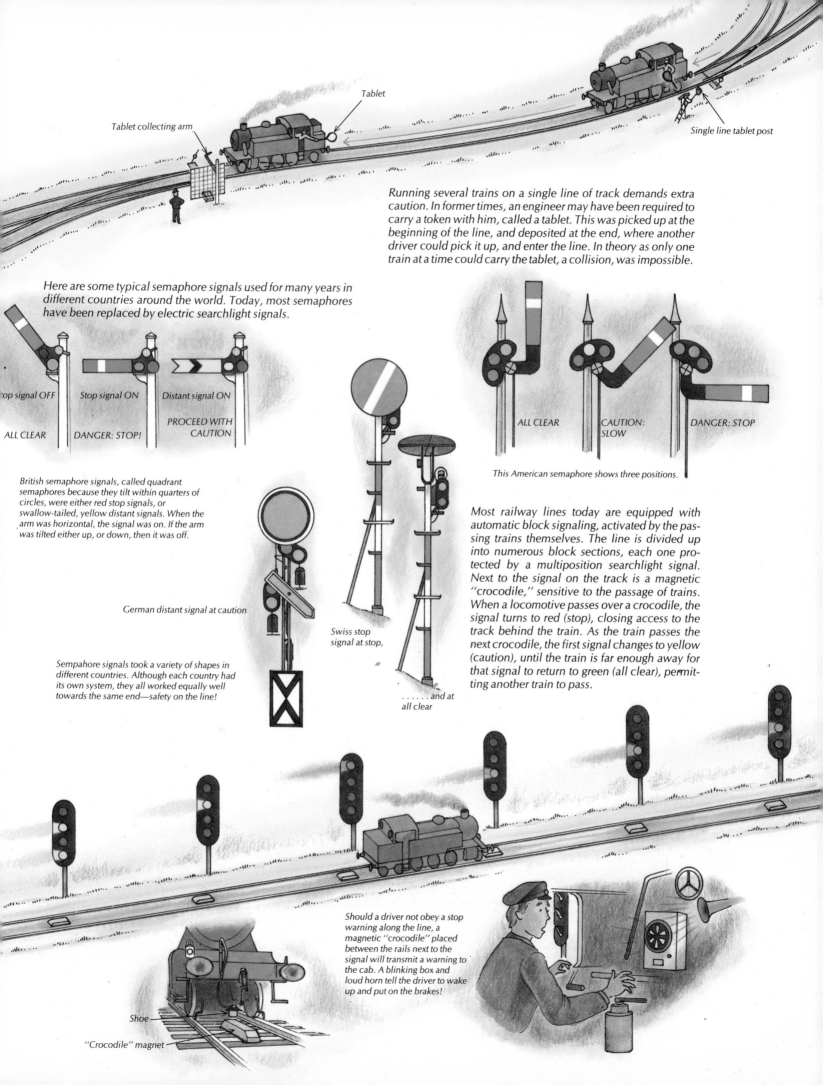

Tablet collecting arm

Tablet

Single line tablet post

Running several trains on a single line of track demands extra caution. In former times, an engineer may have been required to carry a token with him, called a tablet. This was picked up at the beginning of the line, and deposited at the end, where another driver could pick it up, and enter the line. In theory as only one train at a time could carry the tablet, a collision, was impossible.

Here are some typical semaphore signals used for many years in different countries around the world. Today, most semaphores have been replaced by electric searchlight signals.

Stop signal OFF

ALL CLEAR

Stop signal ON

DANGER: STOP!

Distant signal ON

PROCEED WITH CAUTION

ALL CLEAR

CAUTION: SLOW

DANGER: STOP

This American semaphore shows three positions.

British semaphore signals, called quadrant semaphores because they tilt within quarters of circles, were either red stop signals, or swallow-tailed, yellow distant signals. When the arm was horizontal, the signal was on. If the arm was tilted either up, or down, then it was off.

German distant signal at caution

Swiss stop signal at stop,

. . . . . . and at all clear

Most railway lines today are equipped with automatic block signaling, activated by the passing trains themselves. The line is divided up into numerous block sections, each one protected by a multiposition searchlight signal. Next to the signal on the track is a magnetic "crocodile," sensitive to the passage of trains. When a locomotive passes over a crocodile, the signal turns to red (stop), closing access to the track behind the train. As the train passes the next crocodile, the first signal changes to yellow (caution), until the train is far enough away for that signal to return to green (all clear), permitting another train to pass.

Sempahore signals took a variety of shapes in different countries. Although each country had its own system, they all worked equally well towards the same end—safety on the line!

Should a driver not obey a stop warning along the line, a magnetic "crocodile" placed between the rails next to the signal will transmit a warning to the cab. A blinking box and loud horn tell the driver to wake up and put on the brakes!

Shoe

"Crocodile" magnet

Cogs and Cables

Because of the poor adhesion of metal wheels to metal rails locomotives cannot easily climb steep inclines. In order to overcome this a number of different solutions have been devised.

The world's first rack and pinion "cogwheel" railway was built by Sylvester Marsh, up Mount Washington, in America, in 1869. Soon afterwards, in 1871, Niklaus Riggenbach built a cogwheel railway up Mount Rigi in Switzerland. Riggenbach's famous railway started a tradition of mountain railway building throughout the Alps.

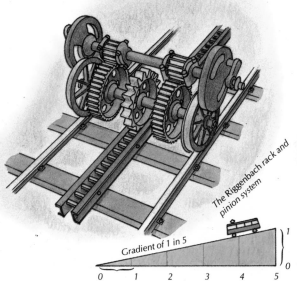

The Riggenbach rack and pinion system

Gradient of 1 in 5

0 1 2 3 4 5

Locomotive "No. 7" of the Vitznau-Rigi railway, 1873

The Riggenbach rack and pinion system is capable of carrying railcars up a gradient of "1 in 5." This means that the railcar will climb one foot higher for every five feet traveled. The rack and pinion system designed by Roman Abt is used today on many mountain railways and can climb grades of 1 in 4. By far the steepest, and most spectacular "cogwheel" railway in the world is that which climbs the Pilatus mountain in Switzerland. This railway uses a system designed by Colonel Edward Locher, and comprises a pair of horizontal cogwheels that grip a central, toothed rail. The cogs' grip makes it unnecessary for the wheels on the pair of outer rails to have flanges, since the train cannot derail from the central rail. Trains on the Pilatus climb gradients of 1 in 2.

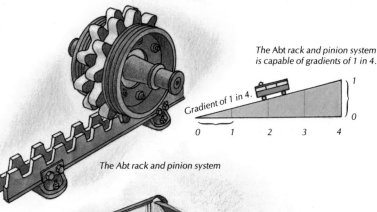

The Abt rack and pinion system is capable of gradients of 1 in 4.

Gradient of 1 in 4.

0 1 2 3 4

The Abt rack and pinion system

The Locher rack and pinion system, capable of gradients of 1 in 2, is used on the Pilatus railway in Switzerland, the steepest in the world.

Gradient of 1 in 2

0 1 2

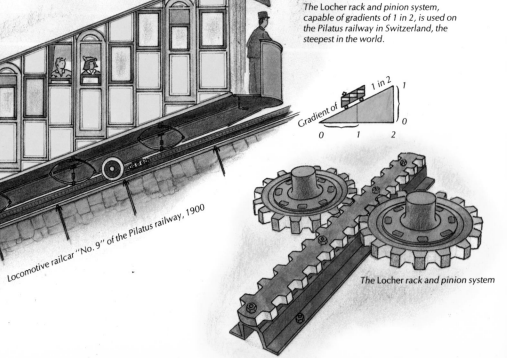

Locomotive railcar "No. 9" of the Pilatus railway, 1900

The Locher rack and pinion system

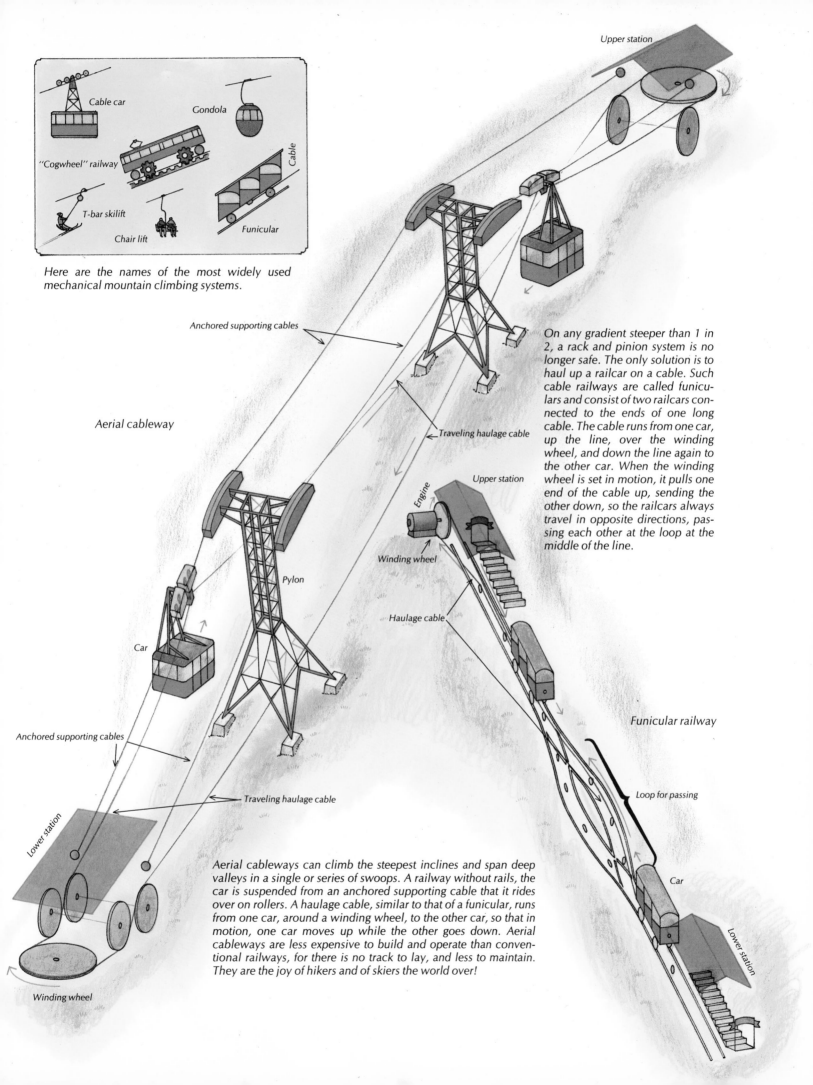

Here are the names of the most widely used mechanical mountain climbing systems.

Cable car

Gondola

"Cogwheel" railway

Cable

T-bar skilift

Chair lift

Funicular

Upper station

Anchored supporting cables

Traveling haulage cable

Aerial cableway

On any gradient steeper than 1 in 2, a rack and pinion system is no longer safe. The only solution is to haul up a railcar on a cable. Such cable railways are called funiculars and consist of two railcars connected to the ends of one long cable. The cable runs from one car, up the line, over the winding wheel, and down the line again to the other car. When the winding wheel is set in motion, it pulls one end of the cable up, sending the other down, so the railcars always travel in opposite directions, passing each other at the loop at the middle of the line.

Engine

Upper station

Winding wheel

Pylon

Haulage cable

Car

Funicular railway

Anchored supporting cables

Loop for passing

Traveling haulage cable

Lower station

Lower station

Car

Aerial cableways can climb the steepest inclines and span deep valleys in a single or series of swoops. A railway without rails, the car is suspended from an anchored supporting cable that it rides over on rollers. A haulage cable, similar to that of a funicular, runs from one car, around a winding wheel, to the other car, so that in motion, one car moves up while the other goes down. Aerial cableways are less expensive to build and operate than conventional railways, for there is no track to lay, and less to maintain. They are the joy of hikers and of skiers the world over!

Winding wheel

Admission, Compression, Ignition, Exhaust

If you have ever looked under the hood of a car, you will doubtlessly have been amazed by the complex picture of twisted pipes, coils of stringy wire, wandering rubber hoses and oddly shaped boxes. It is strange to think that something that looks so awkward can actually propel a car! Yet, for all its complexity at first view, the gasoline engine does in fact work in a very simple way. Let's take a quick look and see how it goes.

The engine is the heart of an automobile. How complicated it looks! Although it is made up of many, different parts, each one does a small, simple job, which helps the engine work smoothly. Of course, should one small piece cease to function, the whole engine may not work. It is little wonder that breakdowns are commonplace! Fortunately, often a small repair to one part will suffice to bring the engine to life again.

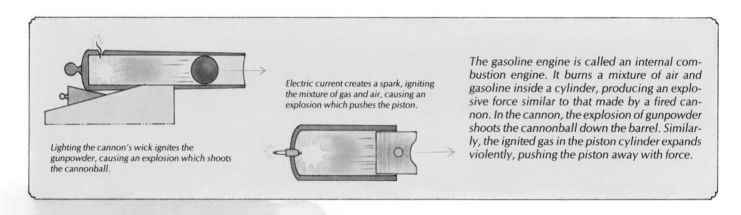

Lighting the cannon's wick ignites the gunpowder, causing an explosion which shoots the cannonball.

Electric current creates a spark, igniting the mixture of gas and air, causing an explosion which pushes the piston.

The gasoline engine is called an internal combustion engine. It burns a mixture of air and gasoline inside a cylinder, producing an explosive force similar to that made by a fired cannon. In the cannon, the explosion of gunpowder shoots the cannonball down the barrel. Similarly, the ignited gas in the piston cylinder expands violently, pushing the piston away with force.

Rudolf Diesel's engine, Augsburg, Germany, 1893

The internal combustion engine was not the invention of one man, but the fruit of experiments and refinements made by a number of enterprising inventors. The Frenchman Alphonse Beau de Rochas is credited with designing the first "four-cycle" engine in 1862. The same year, Jean-Etienne Lenoir designed, on paper, a motor vehicle using a gasoline engine. Niklaus Otto, in Germany, patented a four-cycle engine in 1876. Four-cycle engines are often called Otto-cycle engines. Carl Benz, in 1885, and Gottlieb Daimler, in 1886, both in Germany, built the first gasoline engined vehicles to run successfully. Rudolf Diesel invented a special combustion engine, which bears his name, in 1893. His engines are commonly used in trucks and boats.

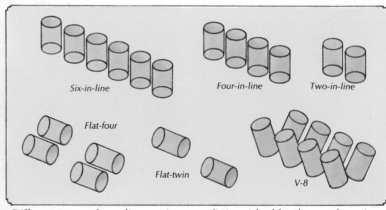

Six-in-line *Four-in-line* *Two-in-line*

Flat-four *Flat-twin* *V-8*

Different types of gasoline engines are distinguished by the number, size, and arrangement of the cylinders. Here are some common engine cylinder arrangements.

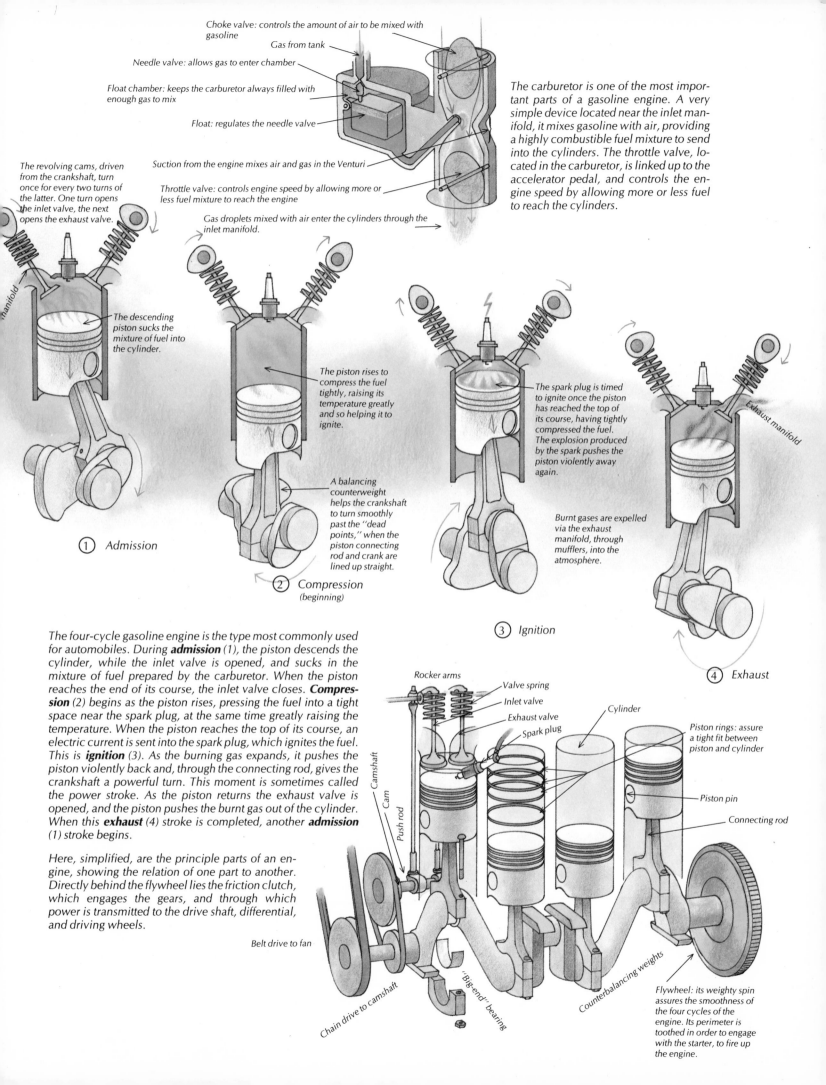

Choke valve: controls the amount of air to be mixed with gasoline

Gas from tank

Needle valve: allows gas to enter chamber

Float chamber: keeps the carburetor always filled with enough gas to mix

Float: regulates the needle valve

The revolving cams, driven from the crankshaft, turn once for every two turns of the latter. One turn opens the inlet valve, the next opens the exhaust valve.

Suction from the engine mixes air and gas in the Venturi

Throttle valve: controls engine speed by allowing more or less fuel mixture to reach the engine

Gas droplets mixed with air enter the cylinders through the inlet manifold.

The carburetor is one of the most important parts of a gasoline engine. A very simple device located near the inlet manifold, it mixes gasoline with air, providing a highly combustible fuel mixture to send into the cylinders. The throttle valve, located in the carburetor, is linked up to the accelerator pedal, and controls the engine speed by allowing more or less fuel to reach the cylinders.

manifold

The descending piston sucks the mixture of fuel into the cylinder.

The piston rises to compress the fuel tightly, raising its temperature greatly and so helping it to ignite.

A balancing counterweight helps the crankshaft to turn smoothly past the "dead points," when the piston connecting rod and crank are lined up straight.

The spark plug is timed to ignite once the piston has reached the top of its course, having tightly compressed the fuel. The explosion produced by the spark pushes the piston violently away again.

Exhaust manifold

Burnt gases are expelled via the exhaust manifold, through mufflers, into the atmosphere.

① Admission

② Compression (beginning)

③ Ignition

④ Exhaust

The four-cycle gasoline engine is the type most commonly used for automobiles. During **admission** (1), the piston descends the cylinder, while the inlet valve is opened, and sucks in the mixture of fuel prepared by the carburetor. When the piston reaches the end of its course, the inlet valve closes. **Compression** (2) begins as the piston rises, pressing the fuel into a tight space near the spark plug, at the same time greatly raising the temperature. When the piston reaches the top of its course, an electric current is sent into the spark plug, which ignites the fuel. This is **ignition** (3). As the burning gas expands, it pushes the piston violently back and, through the connecting rod, gives the crankshaft a powerful turn. This moment is sometimes called the power stroke. As the piston returns the exhaust valve is opened, and the piston pushes the burnt gas out of the cylinder. When this **exhaust** (4) stroke is completed, another **admission** (1) stroke begins.

Here, simplified, are the principle parts of an engine, showing the relation of one part to another. Directly behind the flywheel lies the friction clutch, which engages the gears, and through which power is transmitted to the drive shaft, differential, and driving wheels.

Rocker arms

Valve spring

Inlet valve

Exhaust valve

Cylinder

Spark plug

Piston rings: assure a tight fit between piston and cylinder

Camshaft

Cam

Push rod

Piston pin

Connecting rod

Belt drive to fan

Chain drive to camshaft

"Big-end" bearing

Counterbalancing weights

Flywheel: its weighty spin assures the smoothness of the four cycles of the engine. Its perimeter is toothed in order to engage with the starter, to fire up the engine.

Anatomy of an Automobile

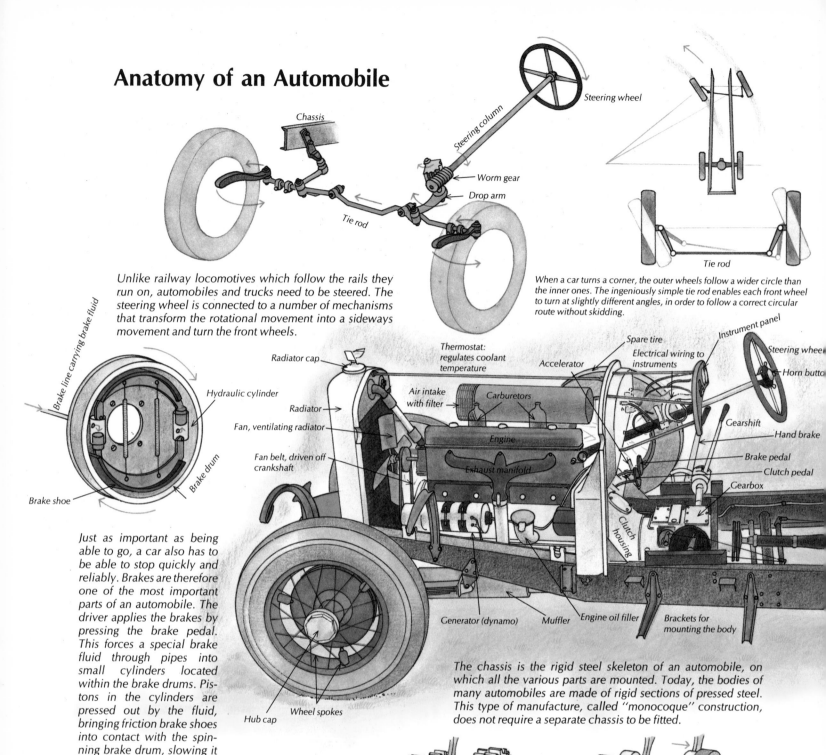

Chassis

Steering column

Steering wheel

Worm gear

Drop arm

Tie rod

Tie rod

Unlike railway locomotives which follow the rails they run on, automobiles and trucks need to be steered. The steering wheel is connected to a number of mechanisms that transform the rotational movement into a sideways movement and turn the front wheels.

When a car turns a corner, the outer wheels follow a wider circle than the inner ones. The ingeniously simple tie rod enables each front wheel to turn at slightly different angles, in order to follow a correct circular route without skidding.

Brake line carrying brake fluid

Hydraulic cylinder

Brake drum

Brake shoe

Radiator cap

Radiator

Fan, ventilating radiator

Fan belt, driven off crankshaft

Thermostat: regulates coolant temperature

Air intake with filter

Carburetors

Engine

Exhaust manifold

Spare tire

Electrical wiring to instruments

Accelerator

Instrument panel

Steering wheel

Horn button

Gearshift

Hand brake

Brake pedal

Clutch pedal

Gearbox

Clutch housing

Generator (dynamo)

Muffler

Engine oil filler

Brackets for mounting the body

Just as important as being able to go, a car also has to be able to stop quickly and reliably. Brakes are therefore one of the most important parts of an automobile. The driver applies the brakes by pressing the brake pedal. This forces a special brake fluid through pipes into small cylinders located within the brake drums. Pistons in the cylinders are pressed out by the fluid, bringing friction brake shoes into contact with the spinning brake drum, slowing it and the wheel down.

Hub cap

Wheel spokes

The chassis is the rigid steel skeleton of an automobile, on which all the various parts are mounted. Today, the bodies of many automobiles are made of rigid sections of pressed steel. This type of manufacture, called "monocoque" construction, does not require a separate chassis to be fitted.

Located between the engine and the drive shaft is the gearbox. Sets of gears allow the wheels to be driven at various speeds in relation to the engine speed. For instance, to move off, or to climb a steep hill, the engine needs extra power, therefore low gears are used so that the engine makes many turns for one powerful turn of the wheel. High gears are used once the automobile has picked up speed, and the gear wheel may turn as fast as, or faster than, the engine speed. Reverse is obtained by moving the gear selector to engage a spur gear on the layshaft with opposite rotation.

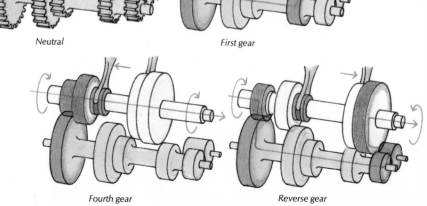

Neutral

First gear

Fourth gear

Reverse gear

An automobile, like the human body, is made up of a great many different organs. The engine is its heart, bringing it to life, while the steering and brakes, like legs and feet, control its movements.

Although, over the years, external design has changed greatly, internally, cars today are still made up of the same basic organs. Let's take a closer look inside.

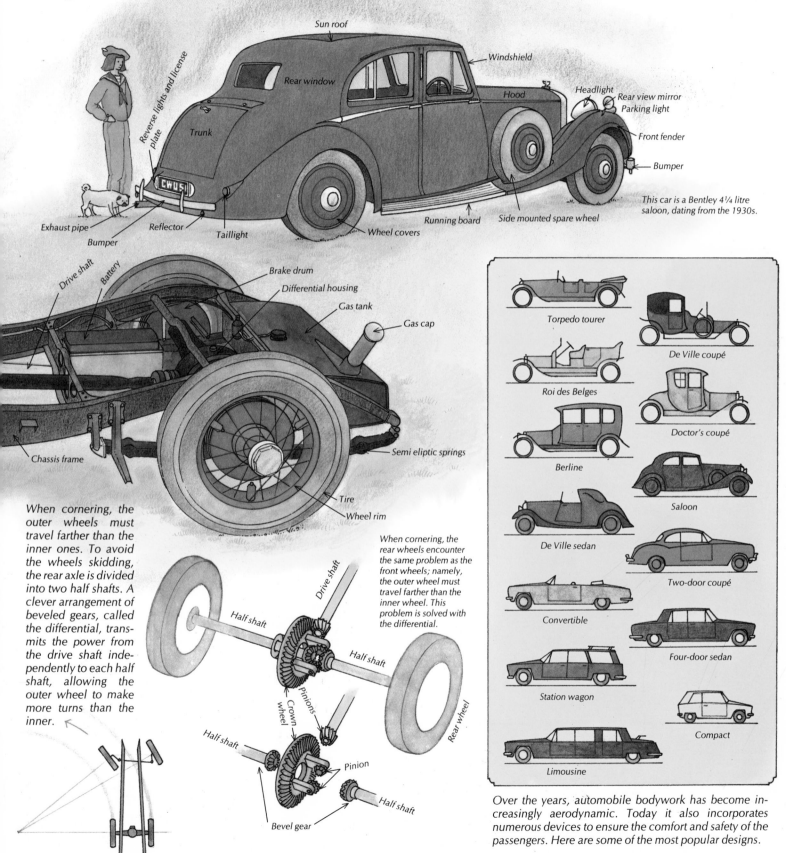

Sun roof

Windshield

Rear window

Hood

Headlight

Rear view mirror
Parking light

Reverse lights and license plate

Trunk

Front fender

Bumper

Exhaust pipe

Reflector

Bumper

Taillight

Wheel covers

Running board

Side mounted spare wheel

This car is a Bentley 4¼ litre saloon, dating from the 1930s.

Drive shaft

Battery

Brake drum

Differential housing

Gas tank

Gas cap

Chassis frame

Semi eliptic springs

Tire

Wheel rim

When cornering, the outer wheels must travel farther than the inner ones. To avoid the wheels skidding, the rear axle is divided into two half shafts. A clever arrangement of beveled gears, called the differential, transmits the power from the drive shaft independently to each half shaft, allowing the outer wheel to make more turns than the inner.

When cornering, the rear wheels encounter the same problem as the front wheels; namely, the outer wheel must travel farther than the inner wheel. This problem is solved with the differential.

Drive shaft

Half shaft

Half shaft

Pinions

Crown wheel

Rear wheel

Half shaft

Half shaft

Pinion

Bevel gear

Torpedo tourer

De Ville coupé

Roi des Belges

Doctor's coupé

Berline

Saloon

De Ville sedan

Two-door coupé

Convertible

Four-door sedan

Station wagon

Compact

Limousine

Over the years, automobile bodywork has become increasingly aerodynamic. Today it also incorporates numerous devices to ensure the comfort and safety of the passengers. Here are some of the most popular designs.

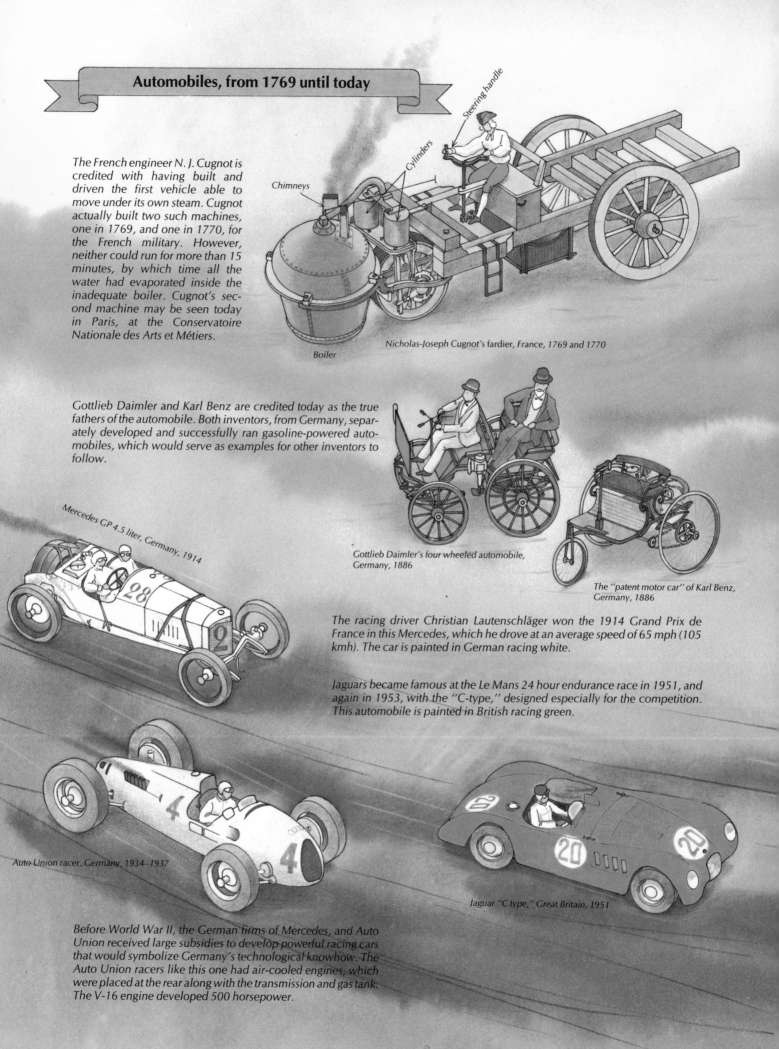

Automobiles, from 1769 until today

The French engineer N. J. Cugnot is credited with having built and driven the first vehicle able to move under its own steam. Cugnot actually built two such machines, one in 1769, and one in 1770, for the French military. However, neither could run for more than 15 minutes, by which time all the water had evaporated inside the inadequate boiler. Cugnot's second machine may be seen today in Paris, at the Conservatoire Nationale des Arts et Métiers.

Chimneys

Cylinders

Steering handle

Boiler

Nicholas-Joseph Cugnot's fardier, France, 1769 and 1770

Gottlieb Daimler and Karl Benz are credited today as the true fathers of the automobile. Both inventors, from Germany, separately developed and successfully ran gasoline-powered automobiles, which would serve as examples for other inventors to follow.

Mercedes GP 4.5 liter, Germany, 1914

Gottlieb Daimler's four wheeled automobile, Germany, 1886

The "patent motor car" of Karl Benz, Germany, 1886

The racing driver Christian Lautenschläger won the 1914 Grand Prix de France in this Mercedes, which he drove at an average speed of 65 mph (105 kmh). The car is painted in German racing white.

Jaguars became famous at the Le Mans 24 hour endurance race in 1951, and again in 1953, with the "C-type," designed especially for the competition. This automobile is painted in British racing green.

Auto Union racer, Germany, 1934–1937

Jaguar "C type," Great Britain, 1951

Before World War II, the German firms of Mercedes, and Auto Union received large subsidies to develop powerful racing cars that would symbolize Germany's technological knowhow. The Auto Union racers like this one had air-cooled engines, which were placed at the rear along with the transmission and gas tank. The V-16 engine developed 500 horsepower.

The inventor of the first railway locomotive, Richard Trevithick, also tested a road locomotive, in 1801. After driving several hundred yards, some mechanical trouble arose. Leaving the machine to celebrate with a meal at a nearby inn, Trevithick returned to find his machine had been completely burnt.

Steam carriage of William Henry James, Great Britain, 1828

Richard Trevithick's "Camborne" road locomotive, Great Britain, 1801

Perhaps the most famous automobile of all is the Ford Model T, manufactured from 1908 to 1927. About 15 million of these sturdy, inexpensive vehicles were made. By 1926, you could buy one new for only $290. Half the automobiles you met on the road were Model Ts.

In the early 1800s, several steam carriages were designed in Britain. However, the Locomotive Act of 1831 required all mechanized vehicles to be preceded by a man on foot, waving a red flag!

In 1934, Citroën built a revolutionary automobile, which remained in production until 1957. It had front wheel drive, a new gear system, hydraulic brakes, and a monocoque body.

Citroën 7S "Traction Avant," France, 1934

Ford Model T, USA, this one dating from 1922

Starter handle

Rear mounted, air-cooled engine

Folding canvas top

Just before the outbreak of World War II, the German government commissioned Ferdinand Porsche to design an inexpensive "people's car." The resulting "Volkswagen," nicknamed "Beetle," went on to be manufactured in millions.

Volkswagen "Beetle," 1953 model, Germany

Windshield

"Jeep," USA, World War II

During World War II, the US Army asked American automobile manufacturers to design a lightweight, four-wheel drive "general purpose" truck. The resulting "GP" truck soon became known as the "Jeep."

Winch

Ford GT "Mark II," USA, 1966

Formula I races are the most important Grand Prix races today. Formula I racers are single seaters and their engine size and body design are subject to special racing rules.

The Ford Motor Company swept up the first three places in the 1966 Le Mans endurance race with a trio of "GTs." Experience gained in racing competitions permits manufacturers to improve the performance, durability, and safety of their standard production cars.

Ferrari Formula I racer, Italy, 1963

Trucks and buses from 1916 until today

Foden "six wheeler" steam tractor, Great Britain, 1916

Before the arrival of powerful diesel-engined trucks in the 1920s, steam-powered tractors were widely used for any heavy tasks, whether they were for transporting, for road building, or for use on the farm.

Ticket conductor

Parisian omnibuses were famed for their open platform at the rear, where one entered the bus and from which one could get a good view of the city while en route. The Schneider "H" buses drove through the streets of Paris between the two World Wars.

Open platform

Refrigerator trucks ensure that any perishables, whether they be meat, fish, fruit, vegetables, or dairy products, are brought from the producer to the stores without any spoilage.

Schneider "Type H" omnibus, France, 1916

Refrigerator unit

co|o-ol

Saurer "D 290," Switzerland

Land Rover, Great Britain

R&O

International Harvester "Transtar 4300," USA

Trucks powered on all four wheels are known as having four-wheel drive. Such vehicles, with their exceptional grip, are handy for reaching places that would normally be inaccessible. The Land Rover, popular worldwide, can be adapted for the most varied tasks.

Big tractor-trailers like this one are a common sight on American highways, where trucks have replaced the railways for much freight traffic.

Trucks and buses do a variety of different tasks, so there are many different types. Here are some common ones.

Van

Tank truck

Tractor-trailer

Pickup truck

Flatbed truck and container

Minibus

Dump truck

Camper

In the United States where children often live miles from school, bright yellow buses carry them to and from home. At bus stops, while school children board or get off, red flashing lights on the roof command other vehicles to halt, allowing the children to cross the street in safety.

Flashing red lights

Wayne-bodied schoolbus, USA

DRINKA PINTA MILKA DAY

London Transport "Routemaster" omnibus, Great Britain, 1950s

One way to carry more people in a bus is to add an extra floor! Double-decker buses are a continuation of earlier horsedrawn omnibuses which had an open-air "imperial" upper deck for passengers. Although many cities have done away with their double-deckers, the London buses have become world famous. A window seat up top is a fine place to see the city!

Renault "GB 231," France

This modern tractor-trailer is a car transporter. The upper decks can be lowered and small ramps extended to allow vehicles to be driven on and off the truck. Transporters are used mainly to deliver new automobiles from the factory to dealers.

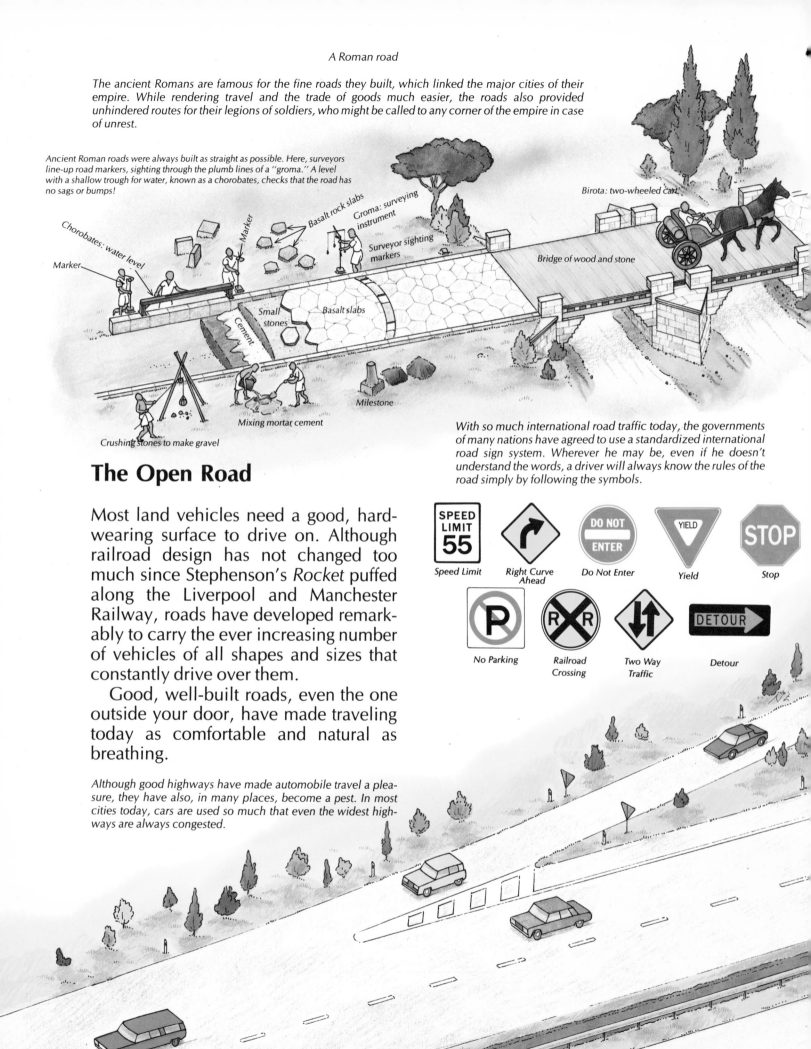

A Roman road

The ancient Romans are famous for the fine roads they built, which linked the major cities of their empire. While rendering travel and the trade of goods much easier, the roads also provided unhindered routes for their legions of soldiers, who might be called to any corner of the empire in case of unrest.

Ancient Roman roads were always built as straight as possible. Here, surveyors line-up road markers, sighting through the plumb lines of a "groma." A level with a shallow trough for water, known as a chorobates, checks that the road has no sags or bumps!

Chorobates: water level

Marker

Marker

Basalt rock slabs

Groma: surveying instrument

Surveyor sighting markers

Birota: two-wheeled cart

Bridge of wood and stone

Small stones

Basalt slabs

Cement

Milestone

Mixing mortar cement

Crushing stones to make gravel

The Open Road

Most land vehicles need a good, hard-wearing surface to drive on. Although railroad design has not changed too much since Stephenson's *Rocket* puffed along the Liverpool and Manchester Railway, roads have developed remarkably to carry the ever increasing number of vehicles of all shapes and sizes that constantly drive over them.

Good, well-built roads, even the one outside your door, have made traveling today as comfortable and natural as breathing.

Although good highways have made automobile travel a pleasure, they have also, in many places, become a pest. In most cities today, cars are used so much that even the widest highways are always congested.

With so much international road traffic today, the governments of many nations have agreed to use a standardized international road sign system. Wherever he may be, even if he doesn't understand the words, a driver will always know the rules of the road simply by following the symbols.

SPEED LIMIT 55
Speed Limit

Right Curve Ahead

DO NOT ENTER
Do Not Enter

YIELD
Yield

STOP
Stop

No Parking

R X R
Railroad Crossing

Two Way Traffic

DETOUR
Detour

After the fall of the Roman Empire, through much of history, road building was carried out in piecemeal fashion with unskilled laborers. For a time in France, every male citizen was required to spend some of his time repairing local roads.

A well built road in the 18th century

Level and sights

Milestone

Quadrant

Well drained roadway with a raise in the middle.

Tamping tool

Fine gravel

Coarse gravel

Large, upright stones

It was only in the 18th century that an applied science of road building took shape. Thanks to the initiative of Pierre-Marie-Jérome Tresaguet in France and to John Loudon McAdam and Thomas Telford, both from Scotland, roads began to be built with care for good drainage, gentle gradients and a firm surface.

Automobiles brought about a radical change in the construction of roads, which from 1905 were covered by a layer of coal tar. As both the number and the speed of automobiles increased, it became necessary to provide them with big, wide highways to drive on. In Italy, in 1925, the first "autostrada" was built between Milan and Varese. Today, networks of highways link major cities all over the world, facilitating trade and travel

A modern highway

Exit lane

"Flyover" bridge

Entry lane

Emergency telephone

Curb

Automobile associations provide breakdown service

Curb markers

Driving lane

Hot asphalt

Roller

Overtaking lane

Paver

Dump truck

Metal crash fence

Center meridian

Road works

Exit lane